100+ IDEAS
FOR TEACHING
THINKING SKILLS

CONTINUUM ONE HUNDREDS SERIES

100+ IDEAS
FOR TEACHING
THINKING SKILLS

Stephen Bowkett

continuum

Continuum International Publishing Group

The Tower Building   80 Maiden Lane, Suite 704
11 York Road   New York,
London   NY 10038
SE1 7NX

www.continuumbooks.com

© Stephen Bowkett 2007   # 76363093

British Library Cataloguing-in-Publication Data
A catalogue record for this book is available from the British Library.

ISBN: 0826483100 (paperback)
        9780826483102

Library of Congress Cataloging-in-Publication Data
A catalog record for this book is available from the Library of Congress.

Designed and typeset by Ben Cracknell Studios | www.benstudios.co.uk

Printed and bound in Great Britain by Ashford Colour Press, Gosport, Hampshire

CONT[ENTS]

INTRODUCTION

SECTION 3   Bringing it all together

100+ IDEAS
FOR TEACHING
THINKING SKILLS

Stephen Bowkett

continuum

Continuum International Publishing Group

The Tower Building	80 Maiden Lane, Suite 704
11 York Road	New York,
London	NY 10038
SE1 7NX	

www.continuumbooks.com

© Stephen Bowkett 2007   # 76363093

British Library Cataloguing-in-Publication Data
A catalogue record for this book is available from the British Library.

ISBN: 0826483100 (paperback)
       9780826483102

Library of Congress Cataloging-in-Publication Data
A catalog record for this book is available from the Library of Congress.

Designed and typeset by Ben Cracknell Studios |
www.benstudios.co.uk

Printed and bound in Great Britain by Ashford Colour Press, Gosport, Hampshire

CONTENTS

SECTION 2 Tools of the game

Thoughts stream through our minds all day long, often without us paying much attention to them. Even when we do notice what's 'on our mind' we might take this mental material quite for granted or, alas, forget most of it without considering how it can be used to our greatest benefit. And yet that very ability to *be aware of our own awareness* is what distinguishes human thought (as far as we can tell) from the mental processes of all other thinking creatures.

The essence of a thinking skills approach to education is that it increases the learners' ability to notice, understand and work more effectively with what goes on inside their own heads. Thinking in all its great diversity, richness and power can be enhanced and more fully enjoyed when students become familiar with and comfortable in using their wonderful 'mental toolbox'. What follows are some suggestions, techniques and strategies that you may find useful in enabling this to happen.

Building the thinking environment

WHAT IS THINKING?

The question has intrigued and puzzled countless people since human beings first started to think! Perhaps the simplest definition is that thinking is what goes on inside our heads. One explanation has it that this is just the outcome of the electrochemical activity of the brain, allowing the organism to survive and hopefully flourish in the world. This rather mechanical view may be accurate enough as far as it goes but does not – yet – account for the astonishing range of human thought, the fact of consciousness, our ability to appreciate beauty, and so on. Aside from this, some argue that the 'machinery' of the brain is only the physical means by which our minds (or personalities, or souls) express themselves. The matter remains unresolved.

Clearly, in the broadest terms, the mental processing we do helps us to make sense of the world. We are 'meaning making creatures', as Marshall McLuhan has said. We have a deep need to know and to understand. This again may come down to the basic fact of survival, or perhaps the nature and power of our thinking are part of a much grander scenario, leading us towards levels of understanding and achievement that we have barely dreamed of.

Who knows? It has been said that the human brain is the most complex instrument in the known universe – so complex that science is only beginning to unravel its mysteries. And this is aside from the more philosophical question of whether such a brain can ever fully understand itself.

ACTIVITY
Encourage students to take a few minutes simply to sit quietly and notice the drift of thoughts through the mind. Ask students to record any observations of the form their thoughts took.

In order to think at all we make use of two fundamental resources, memory and imagination. As we go through life we absorb incalculable amounts of information – and read this word as in-formation: What comes into our heads is continually being formed into greater meanings and understandings.

The point of this in-forming is to create a kind of a blueprint, a map, as it were, of what the world is like and how we as individuals fit into it. This so-called 'map of reality' is not reality, of course, but our subjective impressions based upon interpretations of our own unique experience. Through various means – science, mathematics, etc. – we can reach a common agreement, a consensus view, about what is real. This serves us well, by and large. But on an individual level 'We see the world, not as it is, but as we are', to quote the writer Anaïs Nin.

The map in our head is our memory. This is not the same as recall, which amounts to the strategies we employ to access the map.

Our other great resource is the resource of imagination. This is the ability we have to move mentally beyond the here-and-now. By drawing upon the map of memory and experience we can make mental constructions of things beyond our immediate situation. In other words, we can have ideas – 'mental forms' – of things that do not yet exist. That is the power of human imagination.

ACTIVITY

Ask students to recall some ordinary recent event. What stands out in their memory? And *how* does it stand out (what makes it memorable)? Now invite students deliberately to change the remembered impressions by an act of imagination. If their memory was of a rainy day, for example, turn it into a sunny day. Begin to practise making deliberate changes in finer detail.

It is widely believed that the mind and the body are fundamentally linked. This is aside from profound issues of soul and self and whether our 'essence' survives physical death. Again for practical purposes we can consider that thinking is connected to emotions and physical behaviours and processes. What goes on in the mind affects what happens in the body, and vice versa.

One immediate and powerful implication of this idea is that by learning to think more effectively, we also develop our emotional resourcefulness and the way we react to life's situations. In other words, we boost our ability to respond, which is what 'response-ability' is all about.

ACTIVITY

Ask students to recall, for example, a funny experience and to notice their emotional response. As appropriate, invite recollections that elicit different emotional responses. Ask students to notice which details of the recollection have the greatest effect; for example, is the memory in colour, experienced in the first person, etc.?

Despite the mind-numbing complexity of the brain and the fathomless issues of mentality, self, thought and reality, in order to build a robust and useful thinking environment we might bear in mind a few simple principles:

o To think we use the essential resources of memory and imagination.
o The mind and the body are linked. Thought and flesh affect one another.

These we have already touched upon. Another useful notion is that

o The mind has a conscious part and a subconscious part.

Conscious thoughts are thoughts we know we are thinking at the time we think them, and for reasons we can consider. So, for example, imagine your next meal. You know you are doing that and why (because I just brought the idea to your attention). Also, by an act of will, you can change those thoughts: 'I was going to have a burger, but now I think I'll have a sandwich because that's healthier.'

You have used imagination (drawing information from your map of reality) to create a scenario of something that doesn't yet exist. Such conscious awareness occurs in what has been called *cognitive space*. This is like a mental arena where our 'thinking agenda' is upfront and out in the open. The thinking tools we use in cognitive space are those of reason, analysis, logic – what have been called the 'critical' thinking skills.

However, these are just some of the tools in the thinking toolbox. We also process information in the *subconscious* part of the mind. In using this term I don't wish to suggest that the subconscious is inferior to or less intelligent than the conscious part. It just works in a different way.

Subconscious thinking goes on behind the scenes, outside the realm of our conscious awareness. So, the dreaming we do at night and thoughts and ideas that seem to come from 'out of the blue' during the day are examples of the subconscious mind at work.

ACTIVITY

Ask students to think about how they go about recalling information. Do they try hard to remember? Do they 'give up' and wait for the memory to come? Begin to develop the strategy of having a *clear intent* for a piece of information to become conscious and then noticing when the memory arrives.

Debates about which attributes of the mind correspond with which structures of the brain are bound to be simplistic and probably not very helpful for our purposes. However it's useful to consider that conscious and subconscious areas of thinking represent the activity of the left and right hemispheres of the neocortex, the most recently evolved part of the brain. These parts/attributes have been called the *logic brain* and the *artist brain*.

The conscious thinking of the logic brain is

- ○ Categorical – likes to think in boxes
- ○ Reflective – looks back with self-awareness
- ○ Deliberate – considers the next step
- ○ Linear/sequential – deals bit by bit
- ○ Verbal – uses linear/sequential methods of communication
- ○ Literal – tends to take things for what they are
- ○ Deconstructive/analytical – takes things apart to reach understanding
- ○ Focused attention – we concentrate on a few things at a time
- ○ Ego-focused – our immediate sense of self tends to be a conscious construct
- ○ Effortful – tries to get results

The subconscious processing of the artist brain is

- ○ Boundless – uses the whole 'map of reality' to make meanings
- ○ Freewheeling – builds understanding using all incoming data
- ○ Intuitive – makes 'illogical leaps' to reach new meanings
- ○ (W)holistic/associative – deals with life 'all at once together'
- ○ Nonverbal – communicates using the whole being
- ○ Metaphorical/symbolic – tends to appreciate many levels of meaning
- ○ Reconstructive – likes to build up and synthesize to reach understanding
- ○ Broad in its domain of attention – deals with huge amounts of information constantly

- Multi-focused – through life creates a rich and layered sense of self
- Effortless – results happen without conscious struggle

Effective thinking means using the right tools from the whole toolkit, depending upon the task to be tackled.

ACTIVITY
Discuss with students what kinds of thinking are required for a range of different tasks at school. Develop the discussion by considering how, for instance, creative thinking is/can be encouraged in Maths and Science, or when logical analytical thinking is necessary in English and the Arts. Point out that 'whole brain' thinking makes learning generally more effective.

The map of reality that we have already referred to might also be called the *thoughtscape* – our mental/emotional landscape; the meanings and understandings we have formed up to the present moment. Because mental activity is ceaseless, the thoughtscape undergoes a continual process of change. It is constantly being updated. Most of these updates are likely to be small-scale; reconfirmations of what we already know and believe. Some alterations require us to modify our understandings of the world. We might make insightful leaps and suddenly realize things more deeply, or perhaps come more gradually to a new outlook. Occasionally what we think we know can be challenged at a very deep level, requiring us to make a personal 'paradigm shift' away from what we previously believed to be true. This is sometimes a painful or disturbing process and often people, consciously or subconsciously, resist changing the familiar and comfortable thoughtscape they know. We all strive to maintain a sense of consistency in what we believe. Resisting new information that challenges those beliefs, has been called *cognitive dissonance* by Leon Festinger of Stanford University.

What we know, feel and believe is reflected in what we say. Our words reveal the thoughtscape. The structure and patterns of language, the metaphors that represent our personal reality, are known as the wordscape; our own 'language landscape' which acts as a kind of interface between the inner world of the self and the outside world of day-by-day events. Developing thinking results in a development of language and vice versa.

The very act of thinking, the creation of new connections and networks of understanding, is mirrored in the way in which brain cells, neurones, link up. The hardwiring of the brain at a cellular level amounts to the *brainscape*, and is the physical analogue of the thoughtscape.

ACTIVITY

Look at the way that proverbs act as metaphors linked to beliefs and how, sometimes, can limit them. For instance, *It never rains but it pours* is an extreme generalization. How many students believe that 'it never rains but it pours'?

ALTERNATIVE ACTIVITY

Establish a discussion which draws out students' beliefs. Appoint some students to be 'neutral observers', whose job it is to notice the metaphors that people used to frame their beliefs. Subsequently (and maintaining students' anonymity as appropriate) look at how such metaphors limit or strengthen the underlying beliefs they refer to.

Usually when students read their attention is fixed on the text; they may or may not be aware of the thoughts they're having as their eyes scan the words. The ideas they encounter are 'made sense of' or there might be some confusion, in which case the student stops and thinks further or skips ahead. When reading fiction, imagery is often evoked in the students' minds and when the story is a good one they 'lose themselves' in the adventure and become quite detached from the outside world.

However, even in this case, when the attention is more inwardly directed, the reader may not be noticing the details of his or her mental scenario, nor reflecting how the written material is being processed. Metacognitive reading is the opposite of this, an awareness of what sense is being made of the words on the page, together with the deliberate application of different thinking tools to fully exploit the potential meanings of the text.

ACTIVITY

'Now, Judy,' said Miss Stephens, making a brief tilt of her head toward the passenger in the back seat, 'I really need to know that you are prepared to make some effort.'

So what sense do we make of this sentence? Ask students to consider – What do we know? What can we infer (what do we think we know based on what's there)? What ideas does speculation produce? What might have led up to this scene? What might happen next?

Metacognitive reading is not to be overused – it's intensive and *tiring*. But it is a useful skill to develop in students and highlights the essential difference between asking 'What does the author mean?' and 'What's going on in your head as you read these words?'

METACOGNITIVE READING

CONSTRUCTING REALITY

The educationalist Margaret Meek in her book *On Being Literate* maintains that 'the construction of reality depends upon the understanding of nonsense'. This notion is important. Our 'sense-making' faculties are there to help us survive in a chaotic world where information reaches us as a complex cascade of impressions. Much of the mental processing we do happens subconsciously. Access to the astonishing network of association and meaning that constitutes our memory is quick and usually effortless – we don't need to try and remember things, or to actively decode new experiences by setting them against past ones. When I stand at the kerb ready to cross the road I don't need to reconstruct an understanding of 'traffic' and link it with 'possible danger'. Nor do I need to try and recall what the black and white stripes on the road mean, or ponder the significance of the red or green human figures that light up alternately.

Our students' language reflects their emergent understanding. Even young children know that when they refer to their own legs and to the legs of a table they are not talking about the same thing, though the same noun is used.

Margaret Meek is a powerful advocate of play as a catalyst for learning. She reminds us that through play we can separate what is said from what is meant and still make sense of it.

ACTIVITY

Notice your students' language and reflect on how effectively they are using it to construct their realities. Encourage students to play with language and to notice how shared sense emerges from the nonsense of the words themselves:

o You haven't got a leg to stand on.
o What's on the TV tonight?
o Drink this, it's a great pick-me-up.
o I'm dying for a cup of tea.
o The kettle's boiling.

PRESENT MOMENT AWARENESS

One way of understanding consciousness is to consider it as 'present moment awareness', the ability we have to notice thoughts passing through cognitive space second by second and to change those thoughts deliberately.

This is the simplest way of putting it, of course. Actually things are more complex. Our present moment awareness arises through where the *conscious point of attention* happens to be fixed. It is easy for me to focus my attention on, say, the paperweight in front of me on my desk. In doing so I 'filter out' most of the rest of the room. I may have a peripheral awareness of what's around me although I do not, as it were, notice or attend to it. Conversely I can sit back in my chair and gaze across my study, gathering up a general impression without paying attention to anything in particular.

On the other hand, as I look at the paperweight I might be reminded of the time when I bought it. In this case my attention turns inward as I notice memories evoked by the paperweight.

Or, as I stare around my room, I might consider rearranging my bookcases. Here I am using my imagination to construct a mental scenario of how the room might be in the future, and again my conscious point of attention is fixed inwardly.

Thinking moment by moment is, then, subtle, complex and fast. Being aware of even these simple ideas above might give us pause to consider further when we ask children to give us their 'undivided attention' or to 'think about the problem'. In teaching thinking we need to ensure that our students are more familiar with what their minds can do, and to specify very clearly the kinds of thinking we want them to engage in.

ACTIVITY

Ask students to shut their eyes and create a mental impression of the room they're in. Afterwards, with eyes open, invite them to notice actual details that they missed. Then, focus their attention on the sounds they hear, then on the weight and position of their bodies sitting in their seats. Have students touch pens, pencils and books and focus attention on the weight and texture of these objects. Begin to establish the habit of present moment awareness.

STATES OF MIND

The kinds of thinking we do are reflected in the electrochemical activity of the brain and various states of arousal. When we focus our conscious attention outwards and engage the tools of logic, analysis and reasoning, the brain produces electrical impulses of around 15 to 25 cycles per second called beta waves.

Being relaxed and yet alert is reflected in the production of alpha waves. The so-called *alpha state* is a very powerful learning state. Here we possess all of our conscious faculties, but our attention is divided between input – what we are being told or asked – and output – the mental responses we make. In other words, we are aware of ideas rising from the subconscious resource and can then consciously modify them to frame an answer.

Sometimes we become intensely absorbed by and involved in daydreams, to the point where we lose awareness of the outside world. In this very deep state of reverie (so called by the writer/philosopher Arthur Koestler), we might tap in directly to subconscious processing and experience waking dreams – hypnogogic imagery – which can lead to insightful leaps of understanding (see Idea 12). This is the theta state.

When consciousness itself switches off in sleep, obviously we enter another state of mind characterized by low frequency delta waves. Subconscious activity continues, of course and is often highly productive in solving problems constructed consciously. The old wisdom of 'sleeping on a problem' can often produce startlingly successful results.

ACTIVITY
- Ask students to give you their 'undivided attention' as you tell them a list of words or numbers that you expect them to remember (beta state).
- Play some soothing music and encourage the students to relax to it, noticing the unforced drift of thoughts that pass through the mind (alpha state).
- Encourage students to recall an occasion when they nearly 'dozed off'. Do they now remember any vivid imagery experienced in that (theta) state?
- Do students remember any dreams which seemed crazy at the time, but which later threw light on some issue or problem?

The four phases of going from Uh? to Aha! arose out of the observations of the mathematician Henri Poincaré and were developed by Graham Wallis in his 1926 book *The Art of Thought*. They are

○ *Preparation for having ideas*. This happens informally just by experiencing the world, or it might be highly formalized and systematic through courses of study and research, etc. In terms of creativity and innovation it has long been recognized that 'discovery favours the prepared mind'.

○ *Incubation (or Assimilation)*. This amounts to what is often a long, slow 'cooking' of the problem largely occurring at a subconscious level. Even if we are consciously engaged on a problem, other tools in the toolbox are working on it outside the realm of our conscious awareness. Because of the holistic nature of subconscious processing, we can assimilate huge amounts of information to arrive at solutions, and work on many problems simultaneously.

○ *Illumination*. The Aha! or Eureka! moment when the mental light goes on and we suddenly realize the answer. In other words, we consciously recognize our insight. This often leads to a permanent and maybe profound change in our understanding of the world.

○ *Verification*. This is the testing of the solution against what we already know personally, or against that which is generally known. So, an intuition (inner tuition) about some other person needs to be verified in the outside world: an insightful new theory needs to be proven against an existing body of knowledge.

If children are being asked to solve problems other than by routine and mechanical processes (doing it by the numbers), then the way the creative thinking process occurs needs to be taken into account.

THE FOUR CLASSIC STAGES
OF THE THINKING PROCESS

Look through a book of puzzles for some appropriate examples and ask students to solve them, not by logic and analysis, but by sleeping on the problem or saying 'the answer will come to me'. For instance, what might be the answer to the puzzle *The Martian said, 'All Martians are liars'*? A book full of such puzzles is *The Paradoxicon* by Nicholas Falletta, Turnstone Press, 1985.

Here are some good examples of how solutions are sometimes reached 'irrationally' and not just by working logically and systematically.

One of the classic cases of how subconscious processing and 'inner tuition' can solve consciously posed problems is the story of Friedrich August Kekule's insight into the benzene molecule. Although there is some controversy about what actually happened, the widely accepted version of events is that Kekule's work into benzenes was being hindered because neither he nor anyone else knew its molecular structure. In the summer of 1854 Kekule reports that he fell into a doze – a deep reverie – and dreamed of snakes writhing on the floor in front of him. He anticipated that something significant was about to happen. As that feeling reached a peak, one of the snakes curled round and put its tail in its mouth. Kekule jolted awake 'just knowing' that the benzene molecule was composed of a ring of carbon atoms. (Another version of the tale suggests that as Kekule gazed dreamily into the flames of a fire he seemed to see carbon atoms dancing together in chains and circles.)

Another well-known example of illumination is that of Albert Einstein's insights in 1907 that led to the formulation of his general theory of relativity. Einstein imagined what would happen to a ball inside an accelerating spaceship, and it was this visualization – what Einstein called 'the happiest thought of my life' – that allowed him to work more systematically on the problem. A further often quoted 'thought experiment' of Einstein's is when he fantasized what the universe would look like if he travelled on a light beam.

These and many other such examples, which occur across the whole field of human knowledge, highlight the importance of using 'whole mind thinking' rather than just linear logical reasoning to lead towards greater understanding. In teaching thinking, we must, as Kekule advised, 'learn to dream. . . And then we will find the truth'.

Many other examples can be found in Leslie Alan Horvitz, *Eureka! Scientific Breakthroughs that Changed the World*, John Wiley and Sons, Inc., 2002.

In life we never stop thinking: the brain is active from before birth to the point of death – indeed, death is now medically recognized as meaning the cessation of brain activity. Teaching thinking amounts to exploiting what the brain does anyway, by raising awareness of the range, power and potential of our mental capabilities.

This undertaking moves us away from simplistic models of education as delivering curriculum content to students, which we then require them to reiterate under testing conditions as a measure of what they know. Similarly a thinking skills approach to teaching and learning goes beyond the employment of mechanical, routine mental skills like simple rote learning or working out problems using formulas or other strategies which the students can't fully explain and don't completely understand.

A truly independent, creative, effective thinker is, as the writer David Gerrold says, a 'perpetual notion machine'. Such a thinker knows that her (or his) ideas are valued; that no idea is ever wasted; that you need to have lots of ideas in order to have your best ideas; that the most powerful thinking uses the whole mind, which means that much of the work goes on even though we can't 'see it happening'.

The best thinkers are inquisitive, open-minded, exploratory, questioning, playful, reflective, childlike yet mature. And they do it mainly because it's fun.

Show students video clips or written extracts of interviews with scientists, writers, artists, philosophers, etc., who exemplify the attitude of effective thinking. A few suggestions are:

○ An Interview with David Bohm, Mystic Fire Video, (Science and philosophy oriented for KS3 and above).

○ Richard P. Feynman, *The Meaning of It All*, Penguin Science, 1999 (Science and philosophy oriented for KS3 and above).

○ Arthur. C. Clarke, *Greetings, Carbon-Based Bipeds!* HarperCollins, 2000 (Science and the future oriented for Upper KS2 and above).

○ Ted Hughes, *Poetry in the Making*, Faber, 1986 (Creative writing for Upper KS2 and above).

○ Ray Bradbury, *Zen in the Art of Writing*, Bantam Books, 1995 (Creative writing and thinking oriented for Upper KS2 and above).

PEAK EXPERIENCES

The psychologist Abraham Maslow pointed out in the 1950s that once a person's 'deficiency needs' (food, warmth, shelter, security, sex) have been satisfied, (s)he requires a degree of creative activity to stay optimally healthy mentally, emotionally and physically.

Much of Maslow's previous work had been with sick people (or, as he called them, 'broken people'). To gain more insight into them he decided to study folks who were healthy instead. Maslow found that people who were actively, creatively engaged in their lives were disposed towards moments of 'bubbling happiness' or surges of, sometimes overwhelming, joy. He called these *peak experiences*.

One delightful outcome of this discovery was that when Maslow made such people aware of what was happening to them, they not only had more peak experiences, but *were more able to generate them at will*. In other words, people gained greater control of the positive cycle between creative thinking and feeling good about it. They could guide their own upward spiral of development.

Abraham Maslow termed this behaviour *self-actualization*. His psychology is based on the idea of 'higher ceilings of human nature' and the belief that fruitful thinking and the peak experiences that accompany it are basic to our health as human beings.

ACTIVITY

Help your students to 'anchor' successful thinking and the good feelings that come out of it. A (literally) handy anchor is to rub the little finger and thumb of the non-writing hand together each time a good idea and consequent feeling of pleasure occurs.

○ 'Catch' students when they think successfully and point it out to them as you give sincere praise.
○ Remind them to use their anchor (the example above or one they choose for themselves) at these times.
○ Suggest that when such a positive anchor is established, they can then use it at other times to encourage good ideas and to summon positive feelings in times of stress.

As human beings our basic natural tendency is to move away from the negative towards the positive. We do what we can to satisfy deficiency needs, and if we accept Abraham Maslow's ideas, as outlined in Idea 14, then we need equally to 'make meaning' in order to stay healthy.

A thinking skills approach to teaching and learning can be established more swiftly and powerfully if we presuppose that

○ Satisfying our need to know is necessary for health.
○ All children have imaginations.
○ All children can be enthused.

It is a well-known fact that *expectations determine outcomes*. If we as teachers take the above points as given our positive expectations will communicate themselves to our students and act as a firm foundation for further progress.

Poincaré's creative thinking process from Uh? to Aha! will be accelerated at all levels if we regard enquiry as an adventure. Such an attitude towards learning is not contrary to the all-too-familiar scenario of 'delivering content': if content is regarded as in-formation, then it serves as fuel to fire the imagination, which is the engine that drives the adventure of enquiry.

With this in mind, we need to develop in children, through regularity of practice, the key skills of

○ Exploring
○ Explaining
○ Planning
○ Doing
○ Evaluating
○ Reflecting

ACTIVITY

Play the What If game. Use an example such as 'What if colours changed without warning?' Practise the effective thinking attitude to suggest answers to these questions:

○ What might the world be like?
○ What problems could we face?
○ How will we solve these problems?

ADVENTURE OF ENQUIRY

21

Part of our attitude as teachers is to recognize that children are our primary resource. The word is significant because its meaning becomes clearer as a verb – to re-source, to go back to the source of the learning. Traditionally schooling has taken the form of telling students facts, figures and formulae which they reiterate afterwards as a measure of how much they know. So, as a simple matter of fact, I might teach my students that the Earth is round ('fact' here being defined by the dictionary as a 'thing certainly known to have occurred or to be true; a datum of experience'). But do you find this simple teaching at all controversial? Is the Earth in fact round, or is it spherical? Should I teach that instead? Or should I tell students that the Earth is an 'oblate spheroid', bulging at the equator and flattened at the poles?

Mark Twain once stated that he never let schooling get in the way of his education. Teaching thinking regards education in its original sense of 'drawing out and rearing up'. If I am truly prepared to treat my students as the primary resource for learning, then my aim is to constantly draw out from them the meanings and understandings they have made up to that point. In encouraging them to tell me what sense they make of the world, by valuing their ideas, I help them to be reared up, to stand confidently as creative and independent thinkers.

These vital qualities of encouraging and valuing support the adventure of enquiry. The students are my resource. I must use what they bring into my classroom – their beliefs, attitudes and culture – and feed it back to them positively as I seek to develop their thinking.

This is the principle of utilization.

The principle works 'subliminally', which is to say that students' behaviour will gradually change as you apply it without telling them overtly that you are doing so. Simply by feeding back their ideas and comments as positively as you can will have an effect. Begin practising the principle of utilization today. So, for example, if a student says she feels frustrated at not being able to complete a task, you might suggest that this feeling shows the strength of her desire to do well. This is something you can praise. Or if a student tells you he can't do a task, tell him to imagine how pleased he'll feel when he has completed it.

There is an old Estonian proverb that says, 'The work shows you how to do it.' By this token, accumulating knowledge might help you to learn how to accumulate more knowledge better. But this, I suggest, is an essentially passive and static process. Establishing a thinking classroom means:

o Using the students as the primary resource.
o Creating an ethos of low threat (i.e. eliminating the fear of the wrong answer) and increasing challenge.
o Establishing the adventure of enquiry.
o *As teachers, having the attitude we want the students to have.*

It has long been recognized that students' learning progresses through trial and error, imitation and insight. Trial and error learning (which I always think sounds rather harrowing!) is experiential but can lead to frustration and take an inordinate amount of time. If we as teachers (and parents) build 'thinking skills behaviour' into our teaching, then we act as positive and powerful role models for our students.

In this context it is useful to consider the notion of the *hidden curriculum*. This means the whole context of what children learn in school, above and beyond what we formally teach them. Viewed in this light we can appreciate that the formal curriculum is but the tip of a much bigger iceberg. Students' values, beliefs, sense of identity, emotional resourcefulness, social skills, attitude to learning, etc. are influenced by the environment of the school in many subtle and powerful ways, of which the syllabus and our programmes of teaching form just a small part.

Another aspect of this idea is *osmotic learning*. That is to say, we all absorb huge amounts of information about the world a) subliminally, below the threshold of conscious awareness and b) as a result of initial conscious thinking, but subsequent subconscious processing.

In other words, a vast amount of learning goes on below the surface. We can best guide and accelerate this process of teaching thinking by cultivating an environment that encourages it, and by modelling good thinking behaviour ourselves.

ACTIVITY

Discuss with your students how some learning occurs subconsciously by 'absorption'. Obvious examples are learning to walk and talk. Sometimes also our beliefs, attitudes and expectations form in this way. Ask students to think about and, if appropriate, to talk about beliefs they have related to their own capabilities, for instance as learners. If the beliefs are positive, ask those students to say more about what thoughts and feelings they experience in order to know that they're positive. If the beliefs are negative, suggest that things we experienced in our younger days, which we might now have forgotten about, are helping those beliefs to linger. Further suggest that if these limiting beliefs are the outcome of a story that lies forgotten in their minds, how will they now change the story to turn the beliefs into positive ones?

Another cornerstone of the thinking approach to teaching and learning is the AUC Principle: Awareness, Understanding, Control.

There is a vast range of thinking tools in the toolbox. Effective thinking begins with an increased awareness of those tools and the jobs to which they are suited. Accelerated learning theory advises us that children learn more effectively when they do *metacognition*, which means 'thinking about the thinking you do'. Of course, in order to achieve that students need to notice what's going on in their heads in the first place.

Awareness, therefore, includes not only knowing what kinds of thinking exist, but how different thinkings work, how they feel, how they operate in various contexts.

And so as you set up tasks that engage students' thinking, ask them also *to notice their own mental behaviour*. When they are aware of what they're doing mentally, they will naturally come to a deeper understanding of how that thinking tool works. So, for instance, you show students a picture of a cat and ask them to notice anything about the cat and to tell you what they've noticed. One student might say, 'I think that's an ugly cat.' Your response of, 'That's interesting, you've noticed the cat *and* you've given me your opinion about it' separates out in the student's mind the difference between a pure observation and a value judgement.

This simple example illustrates the important principle of *making thinking explicit*. When a student, through your feedback, understands the difference between, in this case, observation and opinion, she is more able to bring that thinking behaviour under conscious control.

ACTIVITY

Begin to raise your students' awareness of how observations are sometimes automatically followed by value judgements and opinions. Have students notice this in other people (without necessarily making a judgement about it!). Develop the AUC principle by raising students' awareness of how what they say reflects the different kinds of thinking they do. Some examples of observations–opinions I have come across include:

○ It never rains but it pours (This is a generalization built upon negatives).

○ Youngsters today are so unreliable (Generalization made without defining 'youngsters' or qualifying how they might be unreliable, or whether 'oldsters' are any more reliable. . .).

○ It's all the same at the end of the day (Here we have a degree of vagueness which is so extreme that the sentence becomes virtually meaningless. The way to address most observations–opinions is to ask for further evidence and qualification. 'What leads you to say that?' is always a powerful and penetrating question).

THE I'S HAVE IT

To summarize our position so far: powerful thinking can be developed by building the four I's into our teaching/learning programmes.

○ *Immersion*. Creating an environment featuring low threat and increasing creative challenge within a rich field of ideas and language. If we regard our own subject areas as domains of learning and understanding, we need to tempt our students to come in and play. My teaching background is in English – that is the 'learning playground' I want children to enter and enjoy.

○ *Imagination*. Regardless of learning styles and preferences, favoured sensory modalities, social preferences for learning, etc., all students have imaginations – the ability to create conscious mental impressions based upon their pre-existing subconscious map of reality. An ideas and language-rich environment will necessarily enrich students' imagined worlds.

○ *Intuition*. 'Inner tuition', which means guiding and also relying upon and learning from our wonderful subconscious resource. Consciously we can handle only limited quantities of information (the received wisdom is seven plus-or-minus two variables at any one time). Subconsciously we process incalculable amounts of information holistically, across the entire mental map of reality.

○ *Intellect*. This is our faculty for reasoning. It is, as it were, the rider that reins in and guides the energy of the galloping horse of the imagination. The subconscious part of the mind is highly reactive. When we consciously direct the subconscious resource it will work towards our predetermined goals. As we notice the outcomes of subconscious activity (illuminations), we can then further engage our conscious thinking tools to review, refine and realize our ideas.

ACTIVITY

Increasingly regard your subject area and classroom as a 'learning playground'. Engage students' interest with pieces of 'wow' information and your own enthusiasm – *The Guinness Book of Records* is a good starting point for gleaning astounding facts related to your subject area. Maintain high expectations. Focus students' attention on what's actually going on in their heads as they think about what you tell them.

BUILDING BLOCKS OF THE THINKING CLASSROOM

Within the context of the four I's mentioned in Idea 19 we might consider that diverse and effective thinking skills can be boosted in these ways

o Developing sensory acuity; being nosy and noticing what goes on in the outside world, and what happens inside the head (metacognition). It is well recognized that there is a strong correlation between learning and the extent to which the senses are deliberately used.

o Regularity of practice in a range of contexts. In other words, learning thinking by *doing* thinking in lots of ways.

o Fostering a love of thinking by active engagement in a variety of tasks where ideas are valued. To learn something well, love it.

o Being aware that learning occurs on many levels. As well as explicit, formal, conscious teaching having an effect we also learn 'osmotically' on a subconscious level. What and how we learn is also influenced by where and when we learn (environment), how we learn (style, preference, disposition), who teaches us (role models), why we learn (purpose, deep level beliefs and identity).

o Learning is essentially a process of meaning-making, which fundamentally enhances and confirms our sense of identity.

ACTIVITY

Discuss with your students how they prefer to learn. When they think do they make pictures in their heads? Do they like plenty of verbal explanations? Do they like working alone or in groups? Do they appreciate having an overview first, or are they happy just to be given facts and ideas and to build these up into a bigger picture?

(Note: Investigate the work of Barbara Prashnig to learn much more about learning styles: *The Power of Diversity*, Network Educational Press, 2004.)

The word 'education' has its roots in *educare*, to rear, and *educere*, to draw out. Education occurs not by simply telling students what to know, but by giving them strategies for finding out how to know, coupled with a sense of discrimination to consider what's worth knowing and why.

Despite the constraints of the curriculum we can still adopt a 'thinking skills approach' that uses curriculum content as the raw material to fuel the process of thinking. Actually this is a highly effective use of classroom time, because thinking strategies taught in one subject can be applied in others. Furthermore, in guiding students towards thinking more effectively we are developing skills that they can use beyond the curriculum, outside school, throughout their adult lives. It has been wisely said that we are the instruments of our own knowing.

These broad ideas can easily be demonstrated by mentioning the fact that the Earth is round (or an oblate spheroid, see Idea 16). I might challenge my students' thinking by guiding their nosiness. . .

ACTIVITY

o So why do you think the Earth is round?
o When did we discover this? Who discovered this?
o How was it discovered that the Earth is round?
o What did we believe before we found out that the Earth is round?
o How can you test for yourself the idea that the Earth is round?
o Are other planets round? How can we find out?
o Are all objects in space round? If not why not, do you think?

And so on. Early on in the students' learning curve this questioning procedure is teacher-led. As they walk along the road to mastery we notice significant changes in students' behaviour:

DRAWING OUT AND REARING UP

- They will use the motifs (the vocabulary) of the subject more insightfully.
- They will generate the questions for themselves.
- They will be increasingly inventive in finding ways of answering those questions.
- They will deploy their skills across the curriculum and beyond.

When I as their teacher recognize this behaviour in my students, then I know they are well on the way to learning how to learn.

Select a question that you've recently asked your students which you think has relied on a reactive (guess the right answer) response and explore with students how it can be made more diverse, engaging and creatively challenging. One example I came across recently was when a teacher said to her group, 'Remind me of what I told you earlier about how the dinosaurs became extinct at the end of the Cretaceous Period.'

This could be made more proactive and goal-oriented by:

○ Asking students to talk about/investigate the meanings of any words they don't understand (I have been amazed, for instance, by the number of students who can't explain what a dinosaur is).
○ Exploring (through research and imagination) different theories that might cause mass extinction.
○ Asking students to consider why it might be important for them to have this information.
○ Playing a 'what if' game (see Idea 15) by asking 'What if the dinosaurs had *not* become extinct?'

Effective thinking is primarily *active*, motivated and directed as far as possible by the thinker. Even in the dullest classrooms plenty of thinking occurs, but this is usually what Edward de Bono calls reactive (or 'guess the right answer') thinking.

○ It occurs in students but is teacher-led and directed, and is often the product of closed/rhetorical questions.
○ Reactive thinking reflects the teacher's concern to check that the students have remembered 'facts'. A right answer is presupposed by all parties.
○ It relies upon outside authority and usually leads to the restatement of pre-packaged content. It therefore implies a predefined world picture.
○ Reactive thinking is governed and limited by a competitive ethos which is judgemental and exclusive ('Well done, David, you've got the answer right. Stephen, you must try harder next time').
○ It inhibits 'risk-taking' behaviour. Ideas have been called one person's heart in another person's hands. Reactive thinking stifles ideas through fear that they'll be judged, belittled, corrected, etc.

GOAL-ORIENTED VERSUS REACTIVE THINKING

On the other hand, goal-oriented behaviour is essentially:

○ Active and under the individual's control.
○ It uses a wide range of thinking tools elegantly and creatively: it involves planning, anticipation, excitement-in-exploration.
○ Goal-oriented thinking remains focused on the process that leads to an end point, as far as both teacher and students are concerned.
○ It uses both external and internal referents. In other words, it employs outside sources of information plus intuitions.
○ Goal-oriented thinking is rational and realistic, but realizes that what ends up as rational might not start out so. As Einstein said, 'If at first the idea is not absurd then there is no hope for it'.
○ Goal-oriented thinking is driven by commitment and self-belief.

ACTIVITY
Carry out a 'thinking audit' in your classroom. Assess the balance between reactive and proactive learning tasks. Judge the degree to which your students understand goal-oriented thinking.

Although a great deal of mental processing and problem-solving goes on subconsciously, the most powerful thinking occurs when the conscious and subconscious parts of the mind work in tandem, each relying on its own particular strengths.

Consciously we can maintain a clear intent to generate ideas, deepen understanding and solve problems. The subconscious then searches across the map of reality for information that is congruent with that outcome. As we settle into a state of 'relaxed alertness' (the alpha state mentioned in Idea 10) the Big Picture, the grand vision, an overview, comes to mind. This is an outcome that has been prepared and assimilated: the vision is, in Poincaré's terms, an illumination (Idea 11).

The next stage is to realize the dream, to make it real(istic) and achievable. Here we need to engage our conscious reasoning and logic to construct a plan. What will the outcome actually look like and feel like? How will it work? How do the parts fit together?

The plan is our blueprint for action, but once constructed it must be verified. We can ask, What changes might I make for this to be the best plan I can think of? In answering that question we make use of both internal and external referents – our intuition and self-judgement, and outside resources.

The ERV formula reflects different mental and emotional states and shifting balances between the conscious and subconscious resources. It is a useful strategy to bear in mind when guiding students in writing better essays, stories and so on. It is also a life skill that can be much more widely applied.

ACTIVITY
Set the students a task like preparing to go on a holiday. Deliberately focus on the separate phases of imagining where they'd like to go, planning how they'll go about it, then asking each other questions to make their plans more effective.

Thinking strategically leads to the achievement of goals. The point of 'goals' is that they are fixed. If my goal is to complete this book, then that goal will not change of itself, but would require a deliberate act to alter it.

The routes I consider to help me reach my goal are strategies – and that is the point and power of strategic thinking. *Strategies are best thought about in the plural.* So in terms of the goal I've already mentioned, what strategies could allow me to achieve it?

○ I can 'chunk' the task of writing the whole book down into smaller tasks. This helps me to tackle the wood by noticing the individual trees. I can think about one section at a time, then build up the book's overall structure.

○ I might also use the ERV formula (Idea 23). Again I start with the vision, then construct one or more plans so that I can realize it – make it real. Considering how I can test the robustness and effectiveness of each plan allows me to rank them; plan A, plan B. . .

○ I can think about the components of the writing process and play with those until I have a clear way forward. A useful tool is the *Star Check*. Draw a six-pointed star on a sheet of paper and put the Six Big Important Questions around the points: What, When, How, Where, Who, Why. This too is a chunking technique, but coming at the problem from a different angle. Spraying off from each point are the questions I need to answer for me to proceed. How much will I write each day? How many words need to be in each section? How long can I write for and get other necessary jobs done in the day? How will I tackle writer's block?, etc.

○ I can apply specific thinking tools to any of the above.

ACTIVITY

Ask students to imagine that they have a major piece of coursework to prepare for you. The task is not for the students to do that coursework, but to plan in detail how they might go about it by focusing on the points made in Idea 23.

Patterns in our language reveal a lot about the 'thoughtscape', the mental/emotional landscape that gives rise to and helps to maintain our attitudes, beliefs, sense of identity, self-esteem and so on (Idea 6). Language is very telling, frequently in deeper ways than the speaker realizes.

Effective thinking is as much dependent upon high self-esteem, confidence, optimism and curiosity as it is on the application of appropriate thinking tools. Be nosy about what your students say and how they say it, beyond the 'surface content' of what they think they are talking about. Look out for limiting factors revealed in the language. . .

○ *Limiting metaphors*. 'I've hit a brick wall with this problem'; 'I'm in deep water here'; 'I can't seem to get a handle on how to move forward.' One way of intervening is to use the speaker's own metaphors in a more positive way: 'Let's see how we can dismantle that wall – or turn the bricks into marshmallows'; 'There are lots of ways of swimming into the shallows'; 'Handles can be made in many different materials. Let's invent some now.'

○ *All-or-nothing thinking*, where the speaker says that something is either right or wrong, one extreme or another. This pattern is often linked with over-generalizing: 'I never get the answer right'; 'He always picks her instead of me'; 'My ideas never work.' Intervene by asking for instances when this was not so.

○ *Labelling*. A label turns a process into a state: 'I'm a loser.' Intervene by 'verbing it' back into a process or behaviour: 'What's happening to cause this "losing" behaviour?' 'What ways can we think of to over-come it?'

ACTIVITY

Ask students to collect examples of people's language that are examples of the points made above. Explore how these examples can be reframed to become more positive and useful.

PAYING ATTENTION TO LANGUAGE

THE POWER OF ETYMOLOGY

Encouraging students to investigate the origins and multiple meanings of words can powerfully develop their awareness of language. A number of examples that I have personally found to be highly illuminating and useful include:

○ *In-formation*. This turns a body of knowledge – a labelled 'thing' – into a process.
○ *Education* – educere, educare – to draw out and rear up. For me this shifts the emphasis of teaching and learning away from the primary function of me inputting to the students outputting.
○ *Idea*, a mental form. For me this equates with 'ideals', a notion that goes back to Plato's concept of perfect mental forms or ultimate templates. It's a useful metaphor, because forms can be modified, dismantled, rebuilt, played with. . .
○ *Intuition* as 'inner tuition', listening to a wisdom that is deeper and other than conscious rationality.
○ *Realize* – to make real through conscious, deliberate planning.

Another delightful example that I came across recently is that 'lesson' and 'legend' go back to the same root that means 'a wonderful story'. Knowing that immediately sharpens my perspective as to what teaching is all about!

ACTIVITY
Have the students investigate the etymology of learning-related words, or key words of a topic they are currently studying.

We live in a representational world. In the same way that our maps of reality are not the same as reality itself, so 'the word is not the thing' or, to put it another way, the menu is not the meal. Our thinking represents our understanding of the world (and our endeavours to understand further) based on our mental maps. The language we use to express our thinking reflects our meaning-making, our interpretation of how things are, based on our individual experience.

Almost without exception the language we use is laden with metaphor ('laden' itself being a metaphor!). Our personal metaphors reveal clues about our learning styles, about our sensory mental preferences, about our limiting (and liberating) beliefs. Noticing the metaphors we and our students use, and then being adventurous and playful as we explore such metaphors, gives us much more control over our language, thinking and the meanings we make.

'Meta' itself derives from the Greek to mean 'above, beyond, higher than'. We've encountered it in this guise in the word 'metacognition'. This is in one sense 'higher thinking', and in another way it means looking back at our thinking from above, from a higher level of mental activity.

Similarly, metalinguistics is the language we use to reflect upon the language we use; words used to explore words. Kieran Egan, Professor of Education at the Simon Fraser University in Canada, suggests that our thinking evolves through a hierarchy of understandings. Beyond our philosophical, language-framed, understanding of the world we develop an *ironic* understanding, wherein we look back at our mental-linguistic frameworks of reality and challenge them to discover if they serve us as well as they can.

(Source: Kieran Egan, *The Educated Mind*, University of Chicago Press, 1998.)

ACTIVITY

Collect snippets of everyday conversation from the high street, from TV, from each other. Work with your students to tease out the metaphors embodied by these words and phrases.

WHAT ARE METAS FOR?

Any subject area of the curriculum can be understood by its vocabulary. Indeed, some educationalists assert that a subject *is* its vocabulary. The terms that make it up are in this sense *motifs*, constituent features that help to define and describe a larger domain. We might assert that a student understands a subject when she has a conceptual overview of that domain, from its basic principles to its detailed features, and can use that subject's vocabulary elegantly, insightfully and creatively.

The educationalist Margaret Meek calls the process of mastering a subject area in this way 'building a literature'. However, she makes the distinction between functional literacy, where vocabulary is used routinely and reactively, and a more profound literacy where the deep structure of the subject is appreciated and expressed through use of its motifs.

Simple communication of 'facts' and the routine application of formulae do not build a literature. A thinking skills approach stands a much better chance, for here we have a range of mental tools that can be applied as we actively engage with ideas, drawing out from students the meanings they've already made within a given domain. A measure of the extent to which they are active, creative thinkers and 'literate' within a subject is reflected by the number and insightfulness of the questions they ask.

In short, if a child can tell me, based on what I said a week ago, that 'the Moon goes round the Earth' and accepts that as a fact, she has not demonstrated active thinking. If she asks ten questions to challenge and explore that concept, and if some of those questions address what words like 'Earth' and 'Moon' mean, then I know I am succeeding as a teacher.

ACTIVITY

Take a simple statement of fact (such as 'The Moon goes round the Earth') and encourage children to ask as many questions as they can think of under the headings of what, where, when, why, how and who.

Confident knowing couples skills and strategies with an attitude. The attitude is one of feeling comfortable in the presence of ambiguity and uncertainty and not being daunted by confusion. Such an attitude is best nurtured in an environment where thinking is valued, where questions are treasured and where 'I don't know' is seen as a wonderful opportunity to explore how we might find out. The skills and strategies rooted in this attitude, and anchored by it, are what this book is all about.

'Confident knowing' is not the same as understanding, nor is it meant to imply in any sense an arrogant 'I've got the answer' kind of stance. It is more about 'Here I am faced with creative challenges and intellectual demands. So how am I best going to meet them?' Confident knowing is about deciding how to tackle mysteries and discovering what lies behind them and being happy when the 'answers' might end up being more mysteries.

ACTIVITY

Allow students to understand the following insights. Encourage students to apply them at every opportunity.

- o In the face of confusion, keep going. Ask 'How else can I try to make sense of this?'
- o What the words say is not always the same as what the writer means.
- o The meaning we take from words might not be the meaning the writer intended.
- o Different school subjects (or different areas of knowledge) have their own vocabularies, styles and conventions.
- o There is not 'reading' but 'readings'. Text can be read in different ways for different reasons.
- o Value all engagement with text. Celebrate 'meaning making'.

CONFIDENT KNOWING

Tools of the game

The philosopher Alfred North Whitehead once said that 'taxonomy is the death of understanding'. My own feeling is that to distinguish between thinking that is creative and thinking that is critical (in the sense of being analytical) is rather artificial. It's true that the ERV process – Envision, Realize, Verify – begins with more emphasis on subconscious activity with the mind in alpha state (Idea 10), moving towards greater use of conscious deliberation and logical thinking, but this is always part of a process where a range of creative and critical thinking tools contribute to the attainment of the goal.

That said, in this book we'll concentrate more on the so-called critical thinking skills: exploration of creative thinking can be found in the companion volume *100+ Ideas For Teaching Creativity*. For reference, according to Fogarty and Bellanca* the more creative thinking skills are: associating, brainstorming, generalizing, hypothesizing, inferring, inventing, making analogies, personifying, predicting, problem-solving.

A list of more critical/analytical skills follows below. At this stage, before we go into more detail, you might like to consider what you think goes on in the mind when we think in these ways. Also, review some of the tasks you give to your students and pick out the kinds of thinking these tasks involve.

- Analyzing for assumption
- Analyzing for bias
- Attributing
- Classifying
- Comparing and contrasting
- Decision-making
- Determining cause and effect
- Drawing conclusions
- Hypothesizing**
- Predicting
- Prioritizing**
- Problem-solving**
- Solving analogies

* Source: Robin Fogarty and James Bellanca, *Teach Them Thinking*, Skylight Publishing, Illinois, 1986.

** I regard these as being both creative and critical, depending on the emphasis placed upon them.

ACTIVITY

Ask your students to consider what these kinds of thinking actually involve: What goes on in their minds as they consider this list? Explain any terminology that's not clear to them, such as 'assumption', 'bias', 'analogy', etc.

It is very easy to feel a sense of security by teaching facts to students, then testing them to make sure they know those facts. When they give the right answers back to us we can assert that they've learned them.

If you've gone along with my ideas so far then I'm sure you'll question, as I do, that this is what true learning is about. Passive recipients of facts may know a lot, but what do they understand? Personally, I think they have not been educated through building a literature by active engagement and creative exploration of ideas-as-in-formation.

An easy way of shifting the emphasis of teaching and learning in this direction is to use the what-do-we-know triangle (Figure 1):

Figure 1: The What-Do-We-Know Triangle

A statement of fact/an opinion/a concept, etc. is written in the top section of the triangle. Limited space means we have to be concise.

There's more space beneath to write a few things about what we know about the initial fact. In this case 'knowledge' is confirmed by logical argument, recourse

to evidence, or demonstration through experiment –
ideally all three.

Below this we consider what we *think* we know in
relation to the initial fact. Apart from anything else this
part of the activity teases out assumptions we've made,
associations we've created, inferences we've arrived at,
other opinions, ideas, beliefs we've simply accepted
uncritically, and so on.

Realizing these things highlights what we put into the
bottom section of the triangle, which is *what we now want
to find out*. Itemizing these helps us to decide what
thinking tools will be most useful in our further
systematic explorations.

Create the template on A4-size paper – or larger if
you intend the students to explore in greater detail.
Clearly this is not a technique to be used constantly, but
even used occasionally it reinforces the basic strategy of
actively investigating statements presented to us.

ACTIVITY
Discuss with students differences between 'knowing' and
'understanding'. Use the what-do-we-know triangle with
a specific example related to your topic area.

AS A MATTER OF FACT

We hear this phrase often in everyday conversation; it is used to supposedly strengthen an argument or viewpoint. But what is a 'fact'? And how often do we question matters of fact when we encounter them?

A fact is defined (in the *Concise Oxford Dictionary*) as 'a thing certainly known to have occurred or be true' and derives from the Latin for a 'deed' (as in 'after the fact') and 'to make'. One immediate way of engaging with facts, then, is to assess the degree of certainty with which they are known, either universally or personally (if someone tells you something 'as a matter of fact'). Specific strategies include:

o Applying the what-do-we-know triangle.
o Asking the Six Big Important Questions (Idea 24).
o Exploring the etymology of the words used in the statement.
o Clarifying your understanding of the motifs/concepts that make up the statement.
o Using what's called the 'meta model' to ask precise questions in order to elicit specific information about *what the other person means by what they say*, rather than what we take their words to mean.

Encourage the students to make a start in using meta model questioning by using words like 'specifically', 'precisely', 'exactly'. . .

o What exactly do you mean by. . .?
o How, specifically, do you know that?
o What, precisely, are the grounds that lead you to say that is a fact?

Ask students to study a list of statements, such as those below, and consider which are facts and/or how their factual nature (or otherwise) might be uncovered. Discuss whether, say, a historical fact differs from a scientific fact. Encourage students to ask meta model questions to give direction to their further investigations.

o Shakespeare is England's greatest playwright.
o The Second World War began in 1939 and ended in 1945.
o Hydrogen is the simplest element.
o A bird in the hand is worth two in the bush.
o Red sky at night, shepherd's delight. Red sky in the morning, shepherd's warning.
o The South of France is a great place to live.

In an environment where ideas are valued and where effective thinking is encouraged, students develop the confidence to dare to question the received wisdom. One measure of the effectiveness of the thinking skills approach is the deployment of a range of strategies for assessing the information with which we are presented. Apart from the techniques mentioned above, guide students into asking the following questions:

○ How recent is the information? Has it been superseded by other ideas/theories/facts?
○ What is the source of the information? Are there other sources that help verify what we are being told?
○ How is the information presented (see Conventions of Genre and Form, Idea 116)? What is the author's purpose in presenting it that way? To inform, entertain, describe, persuade, etc.? How else could *we* usefully present it?
○ How does the presentation of the information contribute to our understanding?
○ What other purposes might the author have in offering this information?
○ Is the author presenting a point of view? If so, how is the author using information to support it?
○ Does the author present different/opposing points of view? Is the author biased? (see 'Analyzing for Bias', Idea 38).
○ Do the ideas follow on logically? (Can we track their 'reasoned relationship'?)
○ Does the author support generalizations?
○ Do I understand the information? What questions can I ask to increase my understanding?

ACTIVITY

With reference to a current area of study, ask students to look at an entry in an encyclopaedia and ask the questions above of the information they're given.

The what-do-we-know triangle (Idea 31) and the list of questions above highlight the notion that what we are told is the tip of the informational iceberg. Beneath the surface there lies the *deep structure* of what is being presented. This includes the presenter's agenda, the deletions, distortions and generalizations (that may be intentional or otherwise) that exist in what the author says *and in what we take the information to mean.*

A past trainer of mine lectured with a sign on the wall above him which said, 'I am responsible for what I say, but not for what you hear.' This is good advice. It reminds us that we all carry different maps of reality in our heads and experience life subjectively, representationally, uniquely. An important purpose of teaching thinking is to enable us to express clearly what we mean, and to explore effectively what meanings other people intend to convey – to test our perceptions against their intentions.

One variation of the what-do-we-know triangle divides it into just two segments, the 'what we are told' section and the rest. The peak of the triangle is the surface structure of the communication. Everything below is the deep structure including what the author means and what we make of it all.

ACTIVITY

Try this example with students as an introduction to the technique. . . Draw the triangle, section it off as above, then in the top part write, 'The glass shattered. There was the sound of running footsteps.' Now explore the deep structure by writing in the bottom part:

○ What information can you gather from these sentences?
○ What questions would you ask to learn more?

This simple exercise can be used across the age range, from 'The three little pigs were friends' to 'Truth is within ourselves; it takes no rise/From outward things' (Lord Byron, *Paracelsus*, i).

DEEP AND SURFACE STRUCTURE

OCCAM'S RAZOR AND
THEORIES OF EVERYTHING

Human beings have a deeply ingrained need to know. It is built into our brains. Such meaning-making happens from the earliest times in our lives. According to the educationalist Kieran Egan young children go through a period of *mythic understanding*: to them the world is filled with mysterious events and forces, which need explaining. And so they mythologize, creating stories to put experiences into a meaningful context.

Another educationalist, John Abbott, suggests that young children especially have the wonderful ability to create 'naive theories of everything'. Ask ten children why the sun rises every day, for instance, and you're likely to get a bundle of wonderful explanations in reply. While these are naive ideas, not grounded in diverse experience or a broad knowledge base, they exemplify behaviour which is crucial in the development of powerful thinking.

How well I remember being told by my parents that thunder was made by the clouds bumping together. This sounded reasonable to me and I believed it for quite a long time, until I began to question how masses of water vapour could 'bump together'. In our role as educators our job is not to deny children's explanations, but to encourage them and then lead children towards questioning and verifying their stories.

A useful tool in guiding children towards refining their understanding is the principle of Occam's Razor, which states that (in science at least) the most economic explanation of the facts is always to be preferred. Which is to say the explanation that least invokes mysterious forces or as-yet unknown factors.

This works in many cases, but we should also bear in mind Sir James Jeans' famous advice that 'The universe is not only stranger than we imagine, but stranger than we *can* imagine!'

ACTIVITY

Take a phenomenon such as 'helium-filled balloons float upwards' and invite students to come up with a range of possible explanations. Apply Occam's Razor to sort the explanations in order of 'reasonableness'. If a student immediately comes up with the 'right answer' that helium is lighter than air, ask how that assertion can be investigated. Ask also what we mean by 'air'!

An assumption is a statement made or a conclusion drawn in the absence of evidence. It might also be defined as knowledge or understanding that has been taken for granted in a communication. So if I were to mention now that going into the alpha state allows you to notice consciously effects of subconscious preprocessing, I'm assuming that you've read through the earlier sections of this book and have come across, understood and remembered the terms 'alpha state', 'subconscious' and 'preprocessing'.

Analyzing for assumption is a basic so-called critical thinking skill, insofar as it's common for us to assume that what we intend to communicate is what *is* communicated. But I'll remind you of the epithet that 'I am responsible for what I say, but not for what you hear.' This highlights the idea that each of us sees the world subjectively, that our maps of reality differ in many, and sometimes profound, ways.

The tool of analyzing for assumption is preceded by noticing assumptions in the first place. As a teacher I need to be constantly alert to the possibility that I'm assuming knowledge and understanding in children that is not yet present. I also need to realize that a label is not an explanation. A ten-year-old student recently told me that the basic structure of a story consisted of 'orientation, complication and resolution'. When I asked her what these long words meant she simply shrugged and said, 'I don't know, but Miss told us that was true.'

Right now, of course, I'm assuming you know the meanings of those long words!

ACTIVITY

Ask students to make a list of words from your subject area that they don't fully understand. How far did you as their teacher take their understanding of the words for granted?

ACTIVITY

With your students study a range of TV and magazine advertisements. Pick out the statements that we assume to be true (or that the advertisers *want* us to assume are true!).

IDEA

37

MAKE IT EXPLICIT

Perhaps it is safe to assume that assumptions exist when communication takes place: beneath the surface of what is written or said there lies a deeper structure of meaning, association, intention, etc. The first step in analyzing for assumption is taken by bringing that deep structure to the surface as far as is possible or appropriate. Then look for generalizations, missing or incomplete links between premise and conclusion, any traces of taken-for-granted prior knowledge.

Correct assumptions in the following ways:

○ Ask the Six Big Important questions.
○ Suggest possible scenarios to explain or fill in the 'assumption gaps'.
○ Use the assessment of information tips in Idea 33.
○ Use more connectives to test the logical links between statements: because, therefore, meanwhile, so, etc.
○ Explore the author's intent: What might his agenda be? (see also Analyzing for Bias, Idea 38).
○ Consolidate the above by using the what-do-we-know triangle on page 46.

ACTIVITY

Ask students to review the statement:

> Sending unmanned probes to the planets makes more sense than developing crewed space vehicles.

Bias is the outcome of a subjective worldview. It is the slanting or weighting of statements to support an opinion or accepted model. Bias may be present deliberately, as when we endeavour to persuade; or unintentionally, for example, when we support general ideas that we never challenge, accepting them as unquestionably true.

At this level we are talking about *paradigms*. These are models of reality generally regarded as true, based upon discoveries arrived at scientifically. In this sense 'truth' is something that can be demonstrated (and potentially falsified) by experiment. More enlightened individuals realize that any model of reality is not reality itself – in other words they recognize their own bias/the bias of the paradigm. All too often, however, belief structures, viewpoints, opinions, remain unchallenged. This leads to what has been called a 'hardening of the categories', which in its more extreme forms results in closed-minded scepticism and emotive responses, including hostility, towards different outlooks.

In the same way that we can assume that assumptions exist, so we can take for granted (unless you want to analyze for assumption!) that communications support the world view of the communicator.

Do an initial check on what is written/spoken by looking for:

o Exaggeration and/or understatement
o Emotive words
o Generalization
o Selection of specific examples to support a general outlook
o 'Weighting' or distortion of 'facts'
o Opinion disguised as truth
o Lack of or inadequate recourse to evidence
o Lack of or inadequate reasoned argument and judgement

Ask students to apply the points above to a statement such as:

o Technology has got us into this mess and technology will get us out of it.
o Statistics show that more students than ever before are going on to further education.
o In the last decade the rise of reality TV has coincided with a decline in the overall intelligence of the population.
o A picture is worth a thousand words.

ACTIVITY
Have students practise analyzing for bias by studying articles on the same topic from different newspapers.

FILTERS AND ALLEYS

My feeling is that the notion of bias is one aspect of a larger phenomenon called *perceptual filtering*. Information we absorb is, generally speaking, generalized, distorted and deleted. This is partly to allow for the processing of the huge quantity of sensory data in real time as it enters the head. Furthermore, we filter input in line with what's already 'written' on the map: we seek to find congruence between what we believe the world to be like and the way it seems to be at this moment.

This can lead to an entrenched view of things at all levels. One way of countering this tendency, while highlighting bias, is to consciously assume different perceptual positions.

Select an issue. Argue the case from the viewpoint you currently hold (perceptual position A). Then – perhaps sitting in a different seat – argue it from the opposite viewpoint (B) *with sincerity*, so that an unbiased onlooker would not be able to tell which view is truly yours. Now sit in the position (C) of the neutral observer and appreciate the bias in arguments A and B. This activity works well in class using groups of three students who 'do the rounds' of positions A, B and C.

A linked activity, often used in drama, is called *decision alley*. Take an issue and clarify two opposing viewpoints. Air them with the whole group, then split the class into two smaller groups, each group taking one viewpoint. Have the students each select a statement supporting their view. Line up the groups facing one another. Have a neutral student walk slowly down the alley. The students in the lines whisper their statements one at a time to the walker, who afterwards reveals whether or not her outlook has been influenced.

ACTIVITY
Pick some topical issues from the news and have students practise perceptual positions and decision alley.

ACTIVITY
Ask students to come up with an issue they feel strongly about and then construct a persuasive argument about it from the opposite viewpoint.

We all visualize. We all see pictures in our mind's eye, even when our conscious sensory preference is auditory or kinaesthetic. The map of memory is predominantly visual. To create visual mental impressions deliberately and to manipulate them knowingly develops metacognitive ability. It also leads to the realization that 'making up one's mind' is something that can be done more or less knowingly, precisely and effectively.

ACTIVITY

There are endless activities for practising visualization. See my book *100+ Ideas for Teaching Creativity* for some further examples. In the meantime, try these:

○ Have students work in pairs. Student A asks Student B to visualize a familiar place, say the street where she lives. Now Student A says 'Imagine you're walking down that street. When you come to the first junction, look to the left. What do you see?' Student B describes what she's noticing in her mind's eye. The activity continues along these lines.

○ Incremental changes. Have students imagine, for example, a chair. Describe it in some detail – Let's say it's a swivel desk chair on castors. It's made of chromium-plated tubular steel with a high back and dark blue upholstery. Now suggest changes one by one. Change the upholstery to red. Make the castors larger. Add a small motor drive beneath the seat so that the chair can swivel by itself. Now put yellow dots on the red upholstery. Turn the arms of the chair into polished dark wood with a high varnish. And so on.

○ Impossibilities Incorporated. Encourage students to imagine impossible things. Have them imagine flying pink elephants and describe further details. Imagine shoes that allowed you to walk in the air. Imagine looking at yourself from the outside. Imagine rainbow-coloured clouds (see also Thought experiments [Idea 12]).

Attributing is the skill of teasing out the elements, traits and characteristics of an idea, feeling, object, etc. (always bearing in mind of course that the whole is often more than the sum of the parts). Attributing is useful in exploring the subtlety and complexity of a thing in order to understand it more thoroughly or simply to arrive at a more generally accepted definition. Such a definition then allows us to see if the object so defined is an attribute or example of a larger group.

One way of introducing the tool of attribution in this way to students is by using the bottom-up-top-down staircase (Figure 2). This particular application is useful when discussing the classification of animals. More broadly it highlights the mental technique of *chunking*, which means breaking something down into smaller components or putting components together to create a larger organization.

Figure 2: The Bottom-Up-Top-Down Staircase

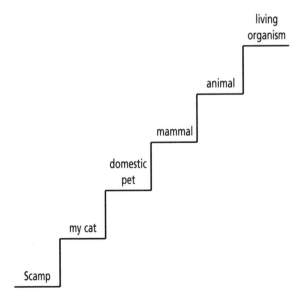

It also helps to develop mental flexibility in encouraging students to take an overview (Big Picture thinking) and then separating out the motifs (constituent features) that help to define and describe that larger domain (logical-sequential thinking). When this mental 'zoom tool' has been mastered to some extent, children will be better able to select the 'chunk size' of the thinking they want to do. So, for example, in story-writing, a student can imagine a narrative overview where she creates a mental impression of the whole tale, or decide to focus in on the mental details that will go into the composition of a single sentence.

ACTIVITY

Have students select a number of familiar objects – a cup, a pencil, a loaf of bread, etc. and list the attributes of each. Then look again for any shared attributes. Can some of these items now be placed into a broader category?

How well I remember, as a young boy in school, working through scores of odd-one-out lists – and being outraged (odd-one-outraged?) when some were marked wrong, despite the fact I had a valid reason for my selection. What would your answer be in this example?

Rose, tulip, daffodil, aconite, ragwort, cornflower

'Rose' perhaps, because it is also the name of a colour, or because it can also be used as a past tense verb? 'Aconite' because it's the only example to begin with a vowel? 'Ragwort' because it's the only one officially listed as a weed that's dangerous to animals? 'Cornflower' because it's the only homophone (cornflour)?

So this exercise can either be used as a game of guess the right answer (reactive thinking, see Idea 22) or more fruitfully as an activity for the practice of attributing, comparing and contrasting (Idea 46) and classifying (Idea 44) within a thinking skills approach to learning. Here are some ways of developing the game:

○ Use picture lists for very young children. Encourage them to notice the attributes of the examples: colour, shape, other physical features. If you used actual flowers you could add smell and texture – but definitely not taste.

○ Make the game more sophisticated by playing odd-two-out using longer lists.

○ Play 'how much odd-one-out'. Have students list as many attributes as possible for each example and judge how closely linked the examples are. For instance, if we decided that one attribute of 'rose' was the great number of cultivated varieties of the flower, then 'tulip' would be closely linked because it too has many types, whereas 'ragwort' would be more distantly linked because (as far as I know) it has no cultivated varieties.

○ Give groups of students a different example from the list and ask them to find as many reasons as they can that make their example the odd-one-out.

○ Play 'odd-one-in'. Have students list attributes that link all of the examples. Use the bottom-up-top-down staircase to make the activity more challenging.

○ Use Venn Diagrams to show shared attributes.

61

IDEA 43

PRACTICE PIECE

Use the lists below to practise and clarify the activities in Idea 42.

○ Beech Elm Violet Fern Orchid Pine
○ Gold Glass Bronze Slate Iron Lead
○ Town City Village Utopia Park Suburb
○ Tea Coke Juice Beer Water Coffee
○ Carpenter Miner Teacher Electrician Baker Barber
○ Ant Bear Cat Deer Eel Fox

Taking a creative approach to handling information generates a variety of ways for using even simple resources like word lists. Try these activities with your students in addition to the ideas above . . .

○ *Creative linking.* Make a link between any two words in the lists. So, for example, 'The carpenter won a gold trophy for his work.' Or 'The teacher's name was Violet.' Develop the activity by using more words from the list in a story.
○ *Filtering.* List items according to your personal preferences.
○ *VAK (Visual, Auditory, Kinaesthetic).* Pick an item from a list and imagine it using all your senses.

Classifying is a pattern-recognition activity. Items are collected that share enough attributes for them to be labelled within the same group. There are many instances where classification is used within the curriculum: hundreds, tens and units in Maths, taxonomy in Biology, parts of speech in English, Dewey Decimal System in Library Studies, etc. As a first step in developing this thinking tool, raise students' awareness of these examples and have them extend the list.   ·

Although classification is regarded as a critical/analytical thinking skill, a creative approach can be taken in its development. Have your students try the following:

o Discuss the concept of uniqueness and where, how and why it applies in certain examples. Can we always pinpoint the particular attributes that make something unique?

o Discuss instances where grouping may be used in a limiting, detrimental or controversial way. Raise awareness of 'hardening of the categories' in terms of generalization, stereotyping, etc.

o Invent new collective nouns for groups – so rather than a 'class' of students a . . .?

o Again use Venn Diagrams to clarify the attributes of a group. Explore the 'overlap areas' where groups are linked.

o Force creative connections between apparently separate groupings. For example, list the attributes of, say, a school and a restaurant. Do any attributes overlap? What would need to change for an overlap to occur? Tease out concepts and use them metaphorically – so, for instance, 'nourishment' could act as a link between the two classifications.

CLASSIFYING

ACTIVITY

Use the accompanying template to help students link the one to the many – the particular to the general. Look back at Idea 41, Attributing. Have students find examples that fit into each category; these can be written in, or you can create a colourful wall display using pictures that the students have drawn for themselves or found in magazines, on the Internet, etc.

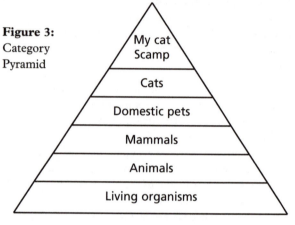

Figure 3:
Category
Pyramid

My cat
Scamp

Cats

Domestic pets

Mammals

Animals

Living organisms

ACTIVITY

Use a category pyramid created by one group as the basis for a game of 20 questions with another group (see also 20 Questions, Idea 75). Begin with a blank template. Tell the students that they have to work out what lies at the tip of the pyramid and all the categories leading up to it. Explain that you know what the categories are and you'll write them in as the questions reveal them. The first category the students have to discover is 'living organisms', so the question 'Is it alive?' would prompt you to label that section of the pyramid. And so on.

Do not allow guesses. The aim of the game is to have students work logically through the categories, from the general to the particular. However, if someone says 'Is it warm-blooded?' before they've established the category 'animal', write 'mammal' in the appropriate place but leave the 'animal' category blank. Students then have to infer the animal category or establish it through logical questioning.

This tool combines attributing and classifying to explore similarities and differences between ideas, objects, feelings, etc. and is a useful way of exploring possibilities, clarifying strategies and making decisions.

The basic steps of the process involve gathering data then sifting it for similarities and differences. Then look for closeness of similarity and scale or degree of difference. So, for example, we see that blood, the Swiss flag and rust can be compared because they all feature red. However this is a 'surface' comparison. At a deeper level we realize that the red of blood and rust are linked because they both indicate the presence of oxygen. Or we might note that both Zorro and Darth Vader are masked and wear black, though I'm sure the differences between them are obvious.

Find instances in your subject or topic area, then gather examples from colleagues by way of highlighting the tool as part of a thinking skills approach. If a comparing and contrasting activity was done in each school subject across one week, it would be very high profile in children's minds. That also holds true for all other thinking skills.

ACTIVITY
(If a cross-curricular exercise is not possible.) Use a broad topic area such as *water*. Ask students to brainstorm that idea and then carry out a comparing/contrasting exercise on the information that's generated.

COMPARING AND CONTRASTING

TAKING IT FORWARD

Develop the skill of comparing/contrasting against more intellectually challenging information.

○ Discuss *levels* of similarity and difference (i.e. deep structure comparisons and contrasts) across a range of contexts. For instance, primates including humans have over 98 per cent of their DNA in common. That is a profound comparison within a discussion of, say, racial or religious differences. Conversely, the eyes of both a human and an octopus work on the same principle but, so the evidence suggests, have evolved independently.

○ Apply the 'good, bad, interesting (or neutral)' tool to add a layer of reasoning and/or judgement to comparisons and contrasts. This is also called the PNI strategy – Positive/Negative/Interesting. So, compare and contrast Indian and Chinese food. Discuss which elements students feel are good similarities/differences and bad ones.

○ Use visual mapping devices to clarify comparisons and contrasts. Venn Diagrams apply here. Also use tree templates – the tree of the evolution of life is one obvious and familiar example.

○ Compare and contrast feelings. Map these on a chart using pleasant/unpleasant for one axis and frequency for another (see Figure 3).

Figure 4: Emotions Map

Ed: the axis titles on the graph (positive/negative) do match the instruction in the last bullet (pleasant/unpleasant)

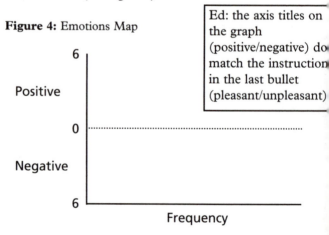

Although decision-making is traditionally regarded as a critical skill that we associate with logic, reasoning and analysis, there is often a powerful subconscious/intuitive element to the process. I daresay that we have all, on occasion, gone with our 'gut feeling' in deciding what or what not to do. If you accept the viewpoint and arguments I offer throughout the book about the subconscious resource then the notion of deciding on a hunch is a valid one, as too is the linked idea of using subjective judgements in making our decisions. However there are occasions, for instance in courts of law, where reasoned argument and the presence or absence of empirical evidence are the bases on which we decide. (Although it's fascinating to compare and contrast the concepts of 'law' and 'justice', and to analyze the linguistic techniques of lawyers which are sometimes anything but objective and impersonal.)

Decisions usually follow the consideration of strategies, 'ways of doing'. Take students through the basic steps in linking strategic thinking with decision-making:

○ Identify the decision that needs to be made.
○ Can the problem or decision be 'chunked down' into smaller and more easily managed parts? If so, prioritize the order in which the parts need to be dealt with (see Prioritizing, Idea 59).
○ List the pros and cons of the options to be decided upon.
○ Explore strategies for reaching a decision (see below).
○ Review your decisions when made. Be sure you understand the reasons why you decided on that option.

ACTIVITY

Use an example such as 'I have £1000 spare money. Should I go on a holiday, decorate my house or buy a new home cinema system?' to allow students to practise decision-making. Follow this up by asking students to come up with examples that apply to themselves.

I USED TO BE INDECISIVE, BUT NOW I'M NOT SO SURE

Help students to practise decision-making by using the strategies below:

o Do a 'Star Check' on the decision to be made (see Idea 24) – the what, where, when, who, why, how of the decision.

o Identify the criteria that influence the decision – that is, the things that are important to you in relation to the decision (the Star Check might tease out some of these).

o Brainstorm possible strategies for reaching a decision:
  – Mind map/spidergram them.
  – Prioritize them in terms of usefulness, effectiveness, cost (time and money, etc.).
  – Balance cost against value.
  – Use the good-bad-interesting tool to help refine the selection of strategies.

o Play the 'Because Game' to clarify your motivations and reasons behind any decision. 'I'm going to wear blue tonight rather than brown because I haven't worn blue for a while. I haven't worn blue for a while because. . .' Just let the because-chain take you where it will. You might discover something new about yourself.

o Play the If-Then game to explore possible consequences of the decision. Set it up like the Because Game.

o If you are still undecided at this point, ask 'What *prevents* me from deciding?' Notice intuitions here, flashes of insight, etc.

o If all else fails, pick out a book at random, select a random page and paragraph on that page. Randomly pluck out a sentence and have the intention that the sentence will help you significantly in coming to the right decision. (This technique relies on subconscious processing.)

o If the answer is not immediately apparent, sleep on the problem.

Determining cause and effect is a useful tool in reaching conclusions and making decisions. It is regarded as a critical thinking skill insofar as cause–effect relationships are often logical and amenable to reason. Certainly in the world of science the robustness of this process has helped build the current paradigm of how the world works (quantum mechanics apart – this area of research has been called 'the dreams that stuff is made from'!).

Begin raising awareness of this thinking skill in students by gathering everyday examples: *If I let go of this glass then it will fall, and maybe it will shatter. . .* Notice, however, that even this ordinary instance is more complex than it first appears, because although we fully expect the glass to fall as an effect of me letting it go, it may or may not shatter. It may bounce and remain intact, or crack, or a piece might chip off. Immediately we need to invoke something like the maybe hand (see Idea 47 in *100+ Ideas for Teaching Creatvity*) to explore and clarify possible outcomes.

When we start to apply the cause–effect concept to people and human relations then we're really walking on shifting sand. . .

ACTIVITY

Take a short story and cut it into chunks. Shuffle the chunks and ask students to put them into what they think is a logical order. Then ask students to discuss in more detail why they think one paragraph or scene comes before the next one in line. (Note that a variation of this activity is to use a comic strip instead of a text-only story.)

DETERMINING CAUSE AND EFFECT

CONSEQUENCE TREES

Decisions are not always straightforward. There may exist any number of variables which, if they come into play, can alter the consequences of an action. If A–then B is the simplest kind of cause and effect: If I let go of this glass then it will fall (see Idea 50). Straightforward logical arguments follow a similar pattern – If–Then–Therefore . . .

If hard work is more likely to bring greater success (A), then therefore you should work harder (B).

More formally the argument looks like this:

o If hard work is more likely to bring greater success, then you should work harder.
o Hard work *does* bring greater success.
o Therefore you should work harder.

This form of argument is called *modus ponens* ('the mode of putting'). It is a *deductive* argument, in that the conclusion arises out of the premises – or to put it another way, the conclusion makes explicit what is already contained in the premises.

The inclusion of 'but' or 'however' complicates things. Working harder brings greater success, but luck plays an important role in this.

We now have a more involved situation. If luck plays a role in success, then simply working harder is not the only strategy or even the best one. If circumstances can be arranged to maximize the effect of luck, then circumstances must be maximized in this way. Maybe the best way to maximize the 'luck effect' is to – option 1, or option 2, or option 3, etc.

We now have logical if–then structures mixed in with inference and speculation. A consequence tree simply makes this kind of thinking more visual (see Figure 5 opposite).

ACTIVITY
Think of some if–then links that allow 'but' or 'however' and encourage students to explore these situations using consequence trees. Here are a few ideas to start you off:

o If everyone were paid the same for their work then equality would no longer be an impossible dream.

- ○ If the three little pigs built a house for the big bad wolf, he wouldn't want to eat them.
- ○ If science leads to greater happiness for more people, then more resources should be put into science.

Figure 5: Consequence Tree

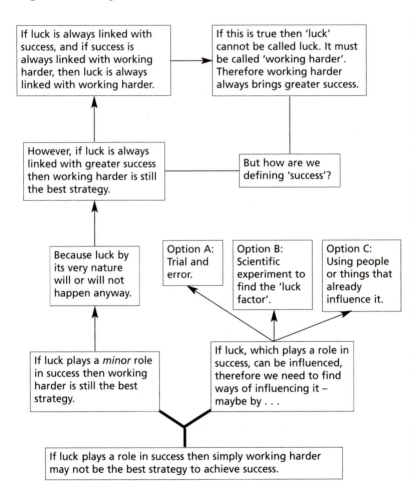

(References: Fisher, Alec (2006) *Critical Thinking: an introduction*, Cambridge: Cambridge University Press/ Weston, Anthony (2000) *A Rulebook for Arguments*, Indianapolis/Cambridge: Hacket)

IDEA
52

ONE WHITE CROW

With reference to determining cause and effect, let me mention the principle of the one white crow. In science hypotheses are firmed up into theories by logical argument, gathering of evidence and experiment. One key aspect of a theory is that it is falsifiable by the same scientific method. If, through ongoing investigation, a theory is not falsified then eventually it is accepted as a physical law and is incorporated into the structure of the currently held paradigm. But science is not a solid bedrock of certainty. There is always more to learn. Our understanding rests on partial truth. So we might accept the law that 'all crows are black'. But it only takes the appearance of one white crow to falsify that theory and send us back to the drawing board.

Educationally this is important. Accelerated learning theory advises that children learn more effectively if they can tolerate ambiguity and uncertainty. This reflects life generally. It allows us to remain mentally flexible in dealing with partial truth, the unexpected and the unknown. The 'chain of events' between If and Then may be invisible, part of the deep structure of how things work. If we accept this we have more strategies for dealing with cause–effect relationships.

ACTIVITY

By way of developing this thinking skill you can:

o Play the If–Then game – clarify the cause–effect link with 'because'.
o Use 'possibility trees' to organize possible outcomes visually.
o Play the 'What-Happens-Next?' game with video clips, books, musical extracts.
o Study chance, coincidence, probability.
o Explore 'alternative histories' – What if the Roman empire had never crumbled?
o Use dramatic role-play to set up situations.

The word conclusion comes from the Latin and means a 'closure', a 'shutting', something that has been drawn together and completed. It is, in one sense, a full stop at the end of a piece of mental work.

There's an upside and a downside to this idea. On a positive note a completion means that I can move on in my thinking. I might conclude, for reasons I've considered, that I'm not suited to a particular job. Therefore I can expand my horizons and look for fresh opportunities. More negatively, I might conclude that John Doe is a crook because he has not honoured the deal we made. This kind of closure acts as a hardening of the categories, which closes off further possibilities. 'A crook' is a *nominalization*, a noun which creates a state (is static) in terms of my thinking and feeling. In many areas of life, therefore, drawing conclusions is helpful if we recognize that as one mental door closes, others open.

Another feature of this kind of thinking is the way in which we arrive at conclusions. We may:

o *Jump to conclusions*. Reach the endpoint without thinking through the steps in between.
o *Intuit*. Reach a conclusion based on outcomes of 'inner tuition', subconscious processing. In this case the hunch or gut reaction is what we recognize (re-cognize, bring to conscious awareness) based on the deep structure of thinking of which we are not aware.
o *Assume*. Draw a conclusion in the absence of reasonable (or any!) evidence.
o *Infer* (from the Latin 'to bring into'). Reach a conclusion based on 'internal referents' and not necessarily using specific external evidence. In this sense we bring our own beliefs, expectations, prejudices, etc. into the equation.
o *Deduce* (from the Latin 'to lead towards', *de+ducere*, 'to lead away'). Move towards a conclusion based on external observed evidence.

DRAWING CONCLUSIONS

Ask students to make a list of statements that they have decided are true. All examples are acceptable, from 'Diamonds are a girl's best friend' to 'Leicester City is having its best ever season' to 'Eating fruit and vegetables is good for you'. Explore with your students *how* they have reached these conclusions.

. . .whatever remains, however improbable, must be the truth. So said Sherlock Holmes, and wise advice it is too. When we employ the thinking skill of drawing conclusions we must be metacognitive as we notice the *process* by which we carry out the work. We can realize that any of the ways of drawing conclusions listed above – from deduction to jumping – can be useful in the appropriate circumstances.

A key question to ask children when they arrive at a conclusion is 'What clues have you noticed that lead you to that answer?' This invites a child to go back and review the details of her observation. Two vital benefits of this process are:

○ The review itself checks the validity of the process of drawing the conclusion.
○ The likelihood that, the second time round, and on reflection, the child will notice more clues to strengthen (or weaken) the initial conclusion.

A refinement of this review question is, 'What clues have you noticed outside? What clues have you noticed inside yourself (in terms of thoughts and feelings)?' In the first place this orients the child's attention outwardly and focuses on observed evidence. In the second place it encourages 'inner noticing', which can reveal the internal information on which assumptions and inferences are based.

Either way, this process allows the child to assemble information and reorder it as necessary so that a pattern of thought forms which leads towards the closure.

ACTIVITY

Use some of the conclusions listed by students for the activity in Idea 53 and apply these key questions:

○ What evidence has led you to that answer?
○ Does that answer 'feel' right?

WHEN YOU HAVE ELIMINATED THE IMPOSSIBLE. . .

A hypothesis is a supposition offered to explain observed facts, or as a basis for reasoning without an assumption of truth. That sounds simple and straightforward enough, but notice how the emphasis is on uncertainty rather than certainty and explanations of facts *as far as we have been able to establish them up to that point*. The Greek root of the word hypothesis is 'foundation' and this usefully allows us to realize that a hypothesis is a platform of explanation on which further rationales are built, again based on observed facts, deductions and logical argument. It is halfway between a pure speculation and a theory (which is a collection of ideas designed to illustrate principles).

Key features to bear in mind when hypothesizing are:

o Begin with a question or statement that gives direction to the subsequent investigation.
o Gather what information is immediately available.
o Generate possible explanations (hypotheses) based on what has been observed.
o Sequence the explanations in terms of, for example, how realistic you think they are at this stage (see Occam's Razor, Idea 35), or how easily you think you can prove or disprove them, etc.
o Clarify and sequence the strategies you can use to prove or disprove the hypothesis.
o Employ the strategies and note the outcomes.
o If the hypothesis is disproved, what other hypotheses now fit the facts? If the hypothesis is not proved, what else needs to be done? What changes need to be made for the hypothesis to fit the facts? (Cycle through this phase as many times as necessary until proof or disproof have been established.)

ACTIVITY

Have students apply the skill of hypothesizing to these (and other) examples:

o Why does the Moon have phases?
o More intelligent people always win arguments.
o The story of Little Red Riding Hood is meant to frighten young children.
o Why does cheese left out in the open go mouldy?

In my opinion hypothesizing is an extension of our childhood ability to create 'naive theories of everything' (see Idea 35). We possess a deep need to understand. Early in life we mythologize. Later our linguistic frameworks coupled with the way we perceive the universe create paradigms, overarching explanations of how things seem to be. Beyond that degree of understanding we can use metacognition and metalinguistics to further test and investigate our belief structures at all levels.

Perhaps the most basic question we can encourage children to ask is *Why?* In an educational environment where ideas are valued, children will feel confident in putting forward explanations that fit the definition of a hypothesis to a greater or lesser degree. Asking a why question each day, and taking a little time to explore possible answers, creates a solid basis for more sophisticated hypothesizing later.

ACTIVITY

Play the Hypothesis Game. Create simple scenarios like the example below. Ask students to offer possible explanations and strategies for gathering more information. Later, get the students to construct scenarios of their own.

- The kitchen window is open.
- The teacloth that covered a plate on the worktop is now on the floor.
- The plate has a few small scraps of cooked chicken on it.
- There are grease marks on the worktop.
- The family cat does not appear when her name is called.

PREDICTING

Predicting is an interesting tool to explore because there are many ways of going about it that involve a range of other thinking skills, from pure guessing, to going with a hunch, to inference, to logical deduction based on observed evidence. In this sense predicting can be classed as both a creative and a critical thinking skill.

Our interest in predicting in all its forms casts light on our human need to control an often unpredictable world. We feel more secure if we can prepare for events we have anticipated. This also raises interesting issues about how – at least in industrialized western cultures – we perceive time. Our view of time tends to be linear-sequential and spatial. We talk of Time's Arrow in science. We imagine the past behind us and the future ahead of us, and our language reflects this. We talk of 'distant memories' and 'the far future'. These are so-called *through time* perceptions. An alternative perception is *in time*, where the conscious point of attention is more focused on the present moment and where the past and future don't exert such a pull on our actions now.

These ideas are relevant in many ways, not least in providing insights into dealing with worry and anxiety, which all too often result from creating scenarios of an imagined future which does not yet, and may never, exist.

ACTIVITY

Ask students to predict what the world might be like in ten years' time, 50 years' time and 100 years' time (pick specific areas of prediction if you wish – computers, schools, shopping, etc.). Encourage students to give reasons for their predictions.

Try these activities when using predicting as a thinking skill. Be aware of the other kinds of thinking that are also used to achieve the result.

58

○ *The If-Then Game* (see Idea 49).

○ *The What-If Game*. Pose a 'what if' to focus on a particular area of enquiry. What if gold suddenly lost its value? What if a small asteroid hit the Earth? (Specify different places to generate different scenarios.) What if a method was discovered of using water as fuel?

○ *Alternative Worlds*. What if dinosaurs had never become extinct? What if America had been discovered a hundred years later than it was? What if the Ancient Egyptians had developed advanced technology?

○ *Future Mapping*. Consider personal futures along a time-line (or using a decision tree template). Mentally leap into the future and notice interesting things. Look back. What steps do I need to take to allow me to reach this point? Use science fiction stories to do future mapping on a large scale.

○ *What Happens Next?* Use video clips or story extracts to work out how the narrative will end. What kinds of thinking did you use to generate an answer?

○ *Play the Fortunately-Unfortunately Game*. 'Unfortunately I dropped a plate. Fortunately it didn't shatter. Unfortunately it cracked. Fortunately it did not land on my foot. Unfortunately it belonged to a set. Fortunately you can buy replacement plates at the local store. Unfortunately the store was closed. . .' One benefit of this game is that it develops the mental flexibility to see the upside and the downside of a situation simultaneously.

○ *Horoscope Language*. Use vague predictive phrases and ask the children to consider how those phrases apply to problems that they identify; to items in the news; to their personal futures, etc. For example:
   – Partnerships are likely.
   – Treasures will soon be revealed.
   – You are on a threshold.
   – An object becomes very important.
   – New areas open up.
   – Notice the seeds of growth.

PRIORITIZING

Prioritizing is the creation of an ordered sequence based on one or more criteria. The word 'criterion' comes from the Greek 'to judge or decide' based on values we have identified. Prioritizing is a useful tool for planning and making decisions. In order to prioritize:

○ Gather all the items to be sequenced.
○ Decide on the criteria you will apply.
○ Prioritize these criteria if necessary!
○ Rank the items using the criteria.
○ Clarify the reasons behind the prioritized items.
○ Review the list and alter the ranking if necessary based on reasons that are clear.

ACTIVITY

Ask students to imagine they need to pack a haversack for a hiking trip. There are lots of things they could take but there is limited room. What items *could* be packed? What criteria will students apply to decide what to pack? What is the most important criterion and why? What is the second most important criterion? And so on. Apply the criteria and rank the items. Make sure students know why they have chosen that order. Review the list.

The deep structure of prioritization games is that they address the wide and complex notion of values, which in turn influence our beliefs and attitudes. These of course contribute powerfully to our sense of identity and purpose (spiritual sense).

I KNOW MY PLACE

ACTIVITIES

○ *Play simple 'gradation games'.* Have the students put items in a sequence based on one or two simple criteria. So – kettle, cup, tub, pail, teapot (based on volume). Extend the skill across the curriculum. Look at the Periodic Table for instance. Study a number of short poems and attempt to rank them according to emotional impact, etc.

○ *Create 'Top Trumps' card games.* Select a category such as 'fictional heroes'. Decide on a number of criteria such as strength, special powers, cleverness, influence over others, etc. Then have students decide on values for these (based on discussion, studying the text) and sequence the heroes on that basis.

○ *Discuss the notion of criteria.* What are values? Introduce the concepts of objective and measurable values (weight, distance, time, etc.) and more subjective, more nebulous (but still vitally important) values such as beauty. Allow your group to explore the notions of subjectivity and objectivity.

○ *Study advertisements.* Have the students prioritize them according to criteria they select.

○ *Look at political speeches and manifestos.* What values are implicit (or explicitly stated) in the text?

○ *Rank scientific inventions* in order of importance (to whom? In what way?).

The world is complex and it is not always possible (or desirable) to rank things in a completely linear way. The tool of Diamond Ranking helps here. Using the template below (Figure 6) and varying it as necessary, items of equal value can be prioritized. You can of course feature as many boxes as you like in any line, although the more you have, the 'thinner' the prioritization becomes.

Figure 6: Diamond Ranking

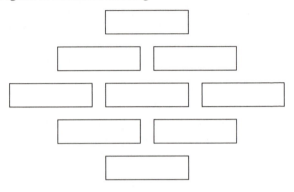

Another handy template is the grid in Figure 7, which applies the principle of diamond ranking without the limitations of the diamond matrix. Figure 7 allows students to rank items against two criteria.

Figure 7: Co-ordinates (Example – Transport plotted for size and speed)

Speed ⟶

Liner				
				Jumbo
		Car		
			Motor-bike	
	Moped			

Size ↑

ACTIVITY

Ask students to rank people's jobs in order of importance, using the diamond ranking tool where possible. *Create different rankings based on different criteria.*

Problems come in many shapes and sizes. A purely critical-analytical approach may be enough to generate a solution. Other problems call more upon our creative imaginations, and may require high levels of emotional resourcefulness, thinking beyond the box and originality. It comes down, again, to choosing the right tools for the right job.

PROBLEM-SOLVING

ACTIVITY

Guide students through the basic problem-solving below:

○ Define a problem as clearly as you can.
○ Check to see if the problem can be broken down into smaller pieces. If so, prioritize the order in which they'll be tackled.
○ Decide what more needs to be found out in order to arrive at a solution.
○ Begin to assemble the thinking tools and strategies that may solve the problem.
○ Look at the problem in different ways. 'Flip the coin'. See it as an opportunity or challenge rather than something that blocks, limits or frustrates. A change of perception can work wonders. Use perceptual filtering more extensively. See the problem through different eyes. 'How would a scientist see this problem? How would Picasso see it? How would Winnie-the-Pooh see it?' etc.
○ Maintain a clear sense of intent that the problem *will be solved*. In other words, exploit subconscious processing.
○ If there is still no solution, move further into the world of metaphor and symbol. If this problem were a national flag, what would it look like? If the problem were a recipe, how would the dish be cooked? If the problem were a person, what conversation would I now have with him/her (and listen for answers).

ACTIVITY

Apply the problem-solving strategy to examples listed in Idea 63.

Below is a list of problems – but feel free to choose your own. Select one or more and have students apply the general strategy from Idea 62. Review the thinking tools you've met so far in this book and try them out as ways toward possible solutions.

○ A family of five people live in a house that's too small for them. They can't afford to move out. Tempers are fraying.

○ The mountainous country of Catalonia is suffering from chronic poverty. It has few natural resources and very little industry. Most people just get by through subsistence farming.

○ A child whom you've identified as gifted in most subjects refuses to make best use of her abilities in school, because she just wants to be 'an ordinary kid'. Her parents are putting pressure on you to 'stretch her further'.

○ You want to write your first book but somehow can't get started.

○ The school has a long-term, worsening, problem of bullying. The Senior Management Team are intent on keeping it quiet.

○ A large asteroid is heading towards the Earth and vast damage will be done if the threat is not averted (I know, you've heard this one before).

'Chunk size' refers to the scale or magnitude of a concept, idea, problem, etc. It forms an important aspect of problem-solving strategies. The point I want to re-emphasize here is that all 'domains' or fields of ideas are made up of many 'motifs', constituent features that help to define and describe that larger domain. Subject areas of the curriculum form one example. A life forms another – the field of time and space within which each of us has an existence.

An overall thinking skill is that of exploring domains by:

o *Chunking down*. Breaking larger chunks into smaller ones – seeing the trees that make up the wood.
o *Chunking up*. Vice versa. Appreciating the Big Picture of the wood by noticing more and more trees in one go.
o *Putting the chunks together in different combinations*. Sometimes a problem or 'stuckness' only exists because we look at its motifs in a certain way.
o *Combining chunks from different domains*. This is truly going beyond the box. Problems can often be solved by gathering insights from different domains and bringing them back to the area in which we need to work. Going beyond the conventions can be a powerful way of reaching solutions.

ACTIVITY

Select one of the problems from Idea 63 and work with students to chunk it down into smaller units. For instance, the problem of the asteroid heading for Earth can initially be chunked down into the possibilities of 1) How can we stop it? 2) How can we cope if it can't be stopped? Each of these scenarios can then be broken down into smaller areas.

Our linear (one word at a time) spoken and written language reflects the fact of our linear-sequential conscious thinking and reveals the need we have to create order in our lives. Sequencing is integrative and is therefore a basic thinking tool that we use in combination with many others to achieve our ends.

Most important in the development of metacognitive skills is the ability to notice the order in which thoughts occur. If we reach a solution, arrive at an opinion, come to a conclusion – what steps did we take to get us to that place?

Any sequencing activity attunes children to the notion that thinking is not random, that it does not just happen. Thinking outcomes are the result of a sequence of mental events: process presupposes order. However, while many sequences follow the basic pattern of beginning-middle-end, they may not be simple lines. . .

ACTIVITY

Ask students to find everyday examples of how sequencing makes life more convenient – the alphabetical listing of locations in an atlas, for instance, or the Dewey Decimal System for organizing non-fiction books.

ACTIVITY

Look at how sequencing and classifying are linked. Ask students to put lists of animals, plants, metals, etc. into a sequence whose logic they can explain.

ACTIVITY

Look at sets of instructions, recipes for instance, and discuss how and why the steps form a logical sequence.

ACTIVITY

Study logical arguments and scientific rationales to appreciate that careful sequencing helps to clarify and persuade.

'Cut-ups' are simply pieces of information written on separate scraps of paper that pupils have then to arrange and organize. The technique in its various guises is an easy but effective way of developing students' discussion skills and teamwork. Depending on the form it takes it gives practice in:

o sequencing and classification
o determining cause and effect
o analyzing problems and arguments
o testing hypotheses
o inference and speculation

Cut-ups can be tailored to suit any level of ability, though in all cases the educational value remains high. Some versions lead to a 'right answer' (the only logical or reasonable arrangement of information), or outcomes might be more open.

ACTIVITY

Some initial ideas for applying the cut-up technique are:

o Cut up a recipe and have students recreate the steps in the correct order.
o Cut a short story into paragraphs or scenes and have students reconstitute the story.
o Take lines from a number of free-verse poems. Encourage students to arrange some or all of the paper scraps to form a new composition.
o Write some statements that, when reconstituted, reveal the order of the planets outward from the sun. So, for example, 'Mars is the next planet outward after Earth.' 'Neptune comes between Uranus and Pluto.' 'Jupiter is the fifth planet outward from the sun,' etc.

LINES, TREES, CYCLES AND MAZES

In developing the skill of sequencing, first collect examples of simple linear sequences for the children to study: number sequences, alphabetical ordering, sets of instructions, plot-lines for stories, time-lines for historical events, and so on.

Now introduce refinements:

○ The Dewey Decimal System in libraries is a number sequence, but increases in complexity with the use of decimal places.

○ Plots for stories feature *subplots*, other sequences of events running parallel with the main action, looping back in one or a number of times. Help children to become familiar with this idea by taking simple stories, fairy tales for example, and creating your own subplots to enrich them.

○ Point out that some sequences are cyclical rather than linear. The water cycle in nature, for example. Study the recycling of different materials. Look at the seasons. Discuss fashion. Explore other notions of 'things coming full cycle', 'what goes around comes around'.

○ Focus on decision trees to emphasize that in many cases, at any point in a sequence there can be multiple outcomes. Link this idea with personal decision-making (see Idea 48).

○ Introduce or develop the idea of flow charts in various contexts: If Yes then go to A, if No then go to B, etc. Look at the popular 'Choose Your Own Adventure' books as a very entertaining example of this.

The technique is to write or draw part of a sequence on a strip of paper and ask students to predict how that sequence might continue. The simplest kind of predictive list would be 1-2-3-4-?-?-? or A-B-C-D-?-?-?. But there are endless variations. Some draw upon memory and prior knowledge, others upon logical reasoning and inference, others upon speculation. Look at Figure 8 'Predictive Strips' below for some examples.

Figure 8: Predictive Strips

Tiny	Small	Sizeable	Big	?	?

Mercury	Venus	Earth	Mars	?	?

In the first case the pattern is clear – increasing size – but there is no single right answer for the missing words in the next two boxes. This realization is itself a valuable one for students to make. In the third example only 'Jupiter' and 'Saturn' will fit, while in the fourth there is the double challenge of working out the pattern (increasing complexity) and finding suitable examples to fill the missing spaces.

Ask students to make their own predictive strips following the examples already given, perhaps with variations:

○ Using the names of villages, towns and cities as places of increasing size.
○ Having each alternate box as a blank.
○ Sequencing the planets in reverse order.
○ Listing gadgets and devices in chronological order of their invention (thus providing a good opportunity for research).

Inductive reasoning is based on observation, past experience, probability and prediction. An inductive argument that 'all crows are black' is constructed thus:

1 The first crow I saw was black. The second crow I saw was black . . . The hundredth crow I saw was black . . .
2 My experience is that all the crows I've seen are black.
3 It is highly probable therefore that the next crow I see will be black.
4 By extension it is probable that all crows are black.

Note that inductive arguments are those where the premises (1 and 2) support the conclusions (3 and 4), whereas in deductive arguments the premises logically entail the conclusions. A deductive argument would be:

1 All crows are black.
2 My pet is a crow.
3 Therefore my pet is black.

However, the conclusion would only be true if all crows *actually were* black. The 'one white crow' idea (see Idea 52) counsels us to caution by stating that if only one white crow were discovered it would destroy the premise that all crows are black and thus invalidate the entire argument.

However, despite this, induction is valuable, because it allows us to form reasonable beliefs about things we have not directly experienced and to make predictions about what the future might be like.

Science often relies upon inductive arguments: even though scientific theories are supposed to be universally true (e.g. for every action there is an equal and opposite reaction), in fact they are usually composed of what we have observed extrapolated further through time and space. They are in fact justified by inductive reasoning.

ACTIVITY
Ask students to assess the likelihood of induced conclusions being true. For example:

o Given the rate of global warming, the rate of species extinction will increase throughout the next century.
o When I next sit down, the chair will support my weight.
o The sun will rise at dawn tomorrow.

MAKING AND SOLVING ANALOGIES

The roots of analogy are to do with proportion, relationship and correspondence. Creating an analogy is a way of expressing one or more of these things often in the form of a metaphor. Analogies are therefore useful for visualizing and clarifying abstract or complex ideas.

Making analogies is perhaps more of a creative skill than it is a critical one, but it prepares the ground for subsequent analysis and exploration. To create an analogy:

○ Focus on the idea for which you want to forge a comparison.
○ Choose the domain from which the metaphor (or simile) will be drawn.
○ Select the motif that will form the correspondence on the basis of one or more similar features.
○ Express the comparison simply:
  – A is like B because they both. . .
  – Or. . . A is to B as C is to D.

ACTIVITY
Suppose, for instance, we wanted to explore relationships between feelings. Ask students to choose motifs from the domain of 'the weather' to forge our analogies.

○ Love is like summer sunshine because they are both full of warmth and light.
○ Rage is to a storm as irritation is to a brief rain shower.

Encourage students to work with analogies and metaphors in the following ways:

○ Rehearse different kinds of relationships that can be expressed analogically.
  – Part–Whole. Word is to paragraph as cog is to. . .
  – Specific–General. Cat is to mammal as pike is to. . .
  – Cause–Effect. Lightning is to thunder as falling is to. . .
  – Item–Characteristic. Water is wet just as rock is. . .

○ Realize there may be many 'answers' to analogies.
  – The mind is a spiderweb because. . .
  – The mind is a rocketship because. . .
  – The mind is a rainbow because. . .
  – The mind is a forest because. . .

○ Create 'off the wall' analogies to stimulate new insights into relationships and generate creative leaps of understanding.
  – Salvador Dali is to art what. . . is to thinking skills.
  – . . . is to education as sunlight is to fruit growing.
  – Basketball is to sport as. . . is to. . .
  – Dancing is like problem-solving because they both. . .

Interfaces encourage relationships between a small number of concepts or items to be explored and developed further. Create a box with four compartments. The dividing lines each mark an interface between two boxes and the items you choose to put inside them.

Earth	Air
Fire	Water

You might use this example geographically and ask students to describe a landscape and/or reaction based on the interface between, say, fire and water or water and earth. Or discuss what types of personality can be represented by the four elements. Combine two elements to create a more complex personality. If two people met, each with a personality represented by an element, how would they react to each other? What would a conversation between them sound like? (And what kinds of thinking allow you to come up with these ideas?). In chemistry, put four chemicals in the boxes and discuss how they would react. In English Language, insert four root words and create some new meanings. Finding ways of using the interfaces idea is itself a creative thinking activity.

Most critical-analytical thinking skills exploit the linear-sequential way of thinking that predominates in the conscious part of the mind (the left hemisphere of the neocortex). While this kind of processing creates a logical order, it may be limiting by creating *only one* sequence and heightens the danger that the student does not think beyond that single 'right answer'. 'Going beyond the given' is a useful definition of creativity. Any device that generates diversity, that encourages alternatives, or that leads the student outside the box to gather fresh insights, adds an extra dimension and power to even the most 'left-brained' kind of thinking.

Many Endings is a simple and versatile technique for achieving this. Whenever a thinking skill generates a linear series of ideas or links, apply the Many Endings tool and see what happens.

ACTIVITY

○ *In English*. Have students take a standard ending such as 'They all lived happily ever after' and suggest others. Study particular stories and think about how else they might end. Are these alternatives satisfactory? Why/why not?

○ *In logic and philosophy*. Play the Because Game/The If-Then Game (Idea 49).

○ *In Biology*. Look at the Top-Down Staircase on page 59. What other steps down from 'mammal' come to mind?

○ *In planning* (such as *future mapping* in Idea 58). Seek alternatives at each step in the plan.

○ *In speculation*. The Many Endings technique builds on the idea of hypothesizing (see Idea 55) and continually opens up possibilities that can then be given attributes or prioritized or analyzed, etc.

'Questioneering' is an attitude which embodies the adventure of enquiry (see Idea 15) and encourages the fruitful combination of tools from the thinking toolbox. It is active and systematic, integrative, in-formative and process based. It is, I suggest, the engine that drives true learning. In the example below, contrast what we might regard as the traditional approach to teaching, by having children 'learn' a fact and recall it at some later time, with the rich field of ideas and thinking strategies generated by questioneering.

Paris is the capital of France

o (Launch question) Why *do you think* Paris is the capital of France?

o How can we find out more to test your ideas?

o When will we know we've got enough information to reach a conclusion?

o What does it mean for a place to be a 'capital'?

o Why do you think capitals are necessary?

o Investigate other capitals. Are some better suited to the purpose, do you think (and why)?

o What other ways can we think of now for deciding on why a place should become a capital?

o What if it were decided to make the capital of France some other place? What are the implications of this idea?

o What other meanings can you think of/discover for the word 'capital'? What new meanings can you create?

Draw out from the students their emergent understandings of how the world works.

Twenty questions has long been an enjoyable party game and is sometimes used as a 'filler' if there are five minutes to spare at the end of the lesson (although it's a big 'if' these days!). However, it is a great technique for sharpening up students' 'questioneering' skills.

ACTIVITY

Refer to the context grid in Idea 98. Pick an item and keep the information to yourself. Show the grid to the group and tell the students that they can ask up to twenty questions to discover which item you have chosen. Allow no guesses, although students can tell you what item they think you have picked if they can justify their answers.

Make a note of the questions as the activity runs and then review them to discover how they could be refined and improved. You will be looking for criteria of quality.

So let's suppose we select item 5/3, the cigarette lighter. High-quality questions in this case would be:

○ Is it smaller than a human hand?
○ Does it have moving parts?
○ Is the item in the top half of the grid? (One student always used this strategy for narrowing down the possibilities. It worked for him every time!)

Short-list the high-quality questions. Decide which ones are effective for the particular item selected and which would work more generally (perhaps after modification). The three questions above remain effective because they address:

○ size
○ degree of complexity
○ coordinates

What other criteria of quality does the game throw up?

Some problems can be tackled by logically working towards a solution: asking the right questions elicits the information needed to solve the puzzle. In other cases no amount of conscious logical effort cracks the nut. However, the answer can 'pop into mind' spontaneously and effortlessly, often accompanied by a feeling of certainty that that answer is indeed the right one.

This experience is the so-called 'eureka moment', a moment of insight where solutions flash into consciousness fully formed. My own belief is that such answers are the result of subconscious processing – for more thoughts on this see my *100+ Ideas for Teaching Creativity*. Other authors, however, are not so sure. David Perkins's *The Eureka Effect: the art and logic of breakthrough thinking* offers a thorough and entertaining survey of the field. An Internet search will also supply many of these so-called 'insight problems'.

ACTIVITY

Put the following problems to your students. Some will have the answers immediately, while others will need to question you further for clues. Notice how some problems are more amenable to 'questioneering' than others.

o Canadian Anthropologist S. P. Beech, after conducting an extensive statistical survey, has found that the average Canadian citizen has one testicle.

o There are three errors in this sentance

o 'A man was having a terrible nightmare. He dreamt he had been taken prisoner during the French Revolution and sentenced to death by guillotine. At the very second the blade fell, the man's wife tapped him smartly on the shoulder to stop his snoring – and the shock killed him instantly!' Why can this story not possibly be true? (Answer: Because if he had really died nobody would ever know what he had been dreaming about.)

o One day Andy says to Brian, 'Hey, I heard this really funny joke from Carl,' and he begins to tell it. But Brian interrupts him. 'Oh, I know that one already.' 'So did Carl tell it to you before?' wonders Andy. 'Oh no,' Brian replies, 'I've never read it or heard it from anyone else.' How is this possible? (Answer: Brian made up the joke originally.)

○ A farmer keeps seventeen sheep in a pen. All but nine escape. How many are left? (Read the puzzle carefully and it's clear that nine, not eight, are left).

THE EXPERT OUTSIDE

Questioneering is one aspect of what I call *quality questioning*. A quality question is ideally created and asked by the student; is driven by a sincere need to know and be further in-formed; acts as fertile soil for a range of further thinking; generates further questions and/or leads to fresh insights that expand horizons of understanding.

A fun game to play with students across the age range is 'the Expert Outside'. Explain that an expert in a particular field will be visiting the class a little later on. (S)he has a very busy schedule, however, and can stay for only five or ten minutes. What questions would you like to ask him/her, bearing in mind there will only be time to ask a few of them?

Have the class generate a list of such questions and then assess them in terms of quality based on the criteria above. Shortlist from the selection, then prioritize the list.

The expert is only pretend, of course, although one teacher I met, who played the game regularly, actually invited real people into the school from time to time. The sense of anticipation that a real expert might be waiting outside the classroom added to the fun of the activity.

A variation on the theme would be to put questions into a search engine on the Internet. Or select another class as the 'collective expert', who will then research for answers.

This creative questioning game can be pitched at any level of sophistication. Make in the first instance a grid of, say, four-by-four boxes. Above each box across the top write the name of a cartoon character, film celebrity, etc. Repeat the names beside the boxes on the vertical axis. Then block out the box where each of the characters intersects on the grid. Supply a copy of the grid to each child or working group.

Suppose we choose Winnie-the-Pooh, Cinderella, Spiderman and the Big Bad Wolf. In the box where, for example, Winnie-the-Pooh and Spiderman intersect, have each student or group think of two quality questions, one coming from Pooh Bear and one from Spiderman. Go through the combinations until all of the boxes contain two questions. That's 24 questions per grid. List them and prioritize them according to the quality questions' criteria.

Develop the activity by replacing cartoon characters with figures from history, famous scientists, contemporary politicians, etc.

WHAT WOULD WINNIE-THE-POOH SAY TO SPIDERMAN?

YIN YANG THINKING

This technique is linked to the perceptual positions and decision alley games (see Idea 39). Yin Yang thinking encourages students to look at both sides of an idea or situation; to realize that things often have both a positive and a negative aspect and to understand that sometimes positives can arise from what seems to be negative and vice versa.

Introduce this technique by showing students the famous Yin Yang symbol. Now play the Fortunately–Unfortunately Game. An example might be 'I tripped over on my way to school. Fortunately. . .' Invite some responses, for instance, 'I didn't hurt myself.' Then say, 'But unfortunately. . .' and collect some more ideas: 'I lost my lunch money'. 'You lost your lunch money? Fortunately. . .'

Develop Yin Yang thinking by asking students to select a motif. This might be a character, real or fictional, a picture icon, a symbol, a concept, a theme, etc.

On a large sheet of paper/a whiteboard draw a line down the middle and draw/write the motif halfway down the line. Designate one half of the sheet as 'negative aspects' and the other as 'positive aspects'. Brainstorm ideas and separate them out into the two areas.

This basic version of the activity creates an overview where a range of opposing ideas is available at a glance (i.e. in the same visual field).

The POV triangle rehearses and refines the technique of perceptual positions (Idea 39) and introduces the PIN technique: Positive, Interesting, Negative.

Have students mark a sheet of paper into three areas. Make one area 'positive', another 'negative' and the third 'interesting'. (Discuss with the students what 'interesting' could mean – possibly neutral, perhaps suggesting potential to be positive and/or negative, etc.).

At the top of the sheet write the name of the object or idea to be studied. This might be something large like 'warfare' or something small and everyday such as 'a tin of baked beans'. Now brainstorm positive, interesting and negative aspects. An immediate outcome for students as they think flexibly in this way is to appreciate that everything has greater potential than might at first be realized.

THE POINT-OF-VIEW TRIANGLE

MEDIATIONS

Younger children especially see the world in extremes. A person is tall or short, thin or fat, good or bad. Tending towards one or other of these *binary opposites* helps children to simplify the complex world around them and make sense of it more quickly. Some fairy tales support this thinking: the big bad wolf is totally bad; the woodsman is the ultimate hero. As we grow, however, most of us come to realize that these extremes rarely exist in reality, and that people, ideas, beliefs, etc. fall somewhere along the line between the two poles.

The skill of mediating – finding middle ground – between opposite ends of the spectrum can be developed in a very simple way.

Draw a horizontal line on the board. At one end write 'I completely agree' and at the other end 'I completely disagree'. Take a simple (but controversial) idea such as 'Brussels sprouts taste good' and ask students to decide where on the line their opinion falls. Many children will immediately jump to one extreme view! Now annotate the mediation line by numbering 1–6 along it. Now create a point of comparison. 'Brussels sprouts taste good compared to cough medicine (or lemons, etc.).' Some students will probably mediate their first reaction.

Develop the technique, and students' sophistication in finding middle ground, by using more profound and complex statements: 'It's right that rich people should pay more tax than poorer people.' Encourage students to move perceptually to a different point on the line. How does that imaginative leap affect their feelings, opinions, arguments?

A more sophisticated version of the mediation line than that described in Idea 81 does away with the 1–6 scale. Instead, two potentially opposed or conflicting concepts are placed one at each end of the line. Take for instance the concepts of 'liberty' and 'security'. It has been said that 'The price of freedom is eternal vigilance', which in this case defines the theme of the example we're considering. The balancing of liberty and security is one aspect of what has been called the 'social contract', an imaginary and largely unspoken agreement to trade one off against the other.

ACTIVITY

Using the above as an initial example, discuss with your students how the ideas of liberty and security are related. Begin to explore where along the line individual students would place themselves – In other words, how much security (and define 'security') would a student be willing to tolerate in order to preserve the right to freedom within society. Have students write points supporting their position for or against on scraps of paper, placing these at their chosen point on the line. This in a powerful sense is their 'standpoint'.

Mediation lines used in this way clarify thinking about ethical dilemmas. A useful sourcebook of examples is Martin Cohen's *101 Ethical Dilemmas* published by Routledge.

IDEA

83

THE TEAMWORK TRIANGLE

The POV triangle can also be used in group work. According to some researchers, one facet of our 'thinking personality' is that each of us tends to be an ideas person, an intellect person or a people-oriented person.

An ideas person is good at tapping into the subconscious resource and popping up ideas in great profusion, initially at least with little thought as to how these might be applied, or considering the effects they could have. An intellect person prefers to assemble facts and construct plans. A robust strategy is the most important thing. A people-oriented person tends to focus on effects and consequences, especially in terms of the impact of a plan on people (rather than upon objects).

By running the other activities in this book with your groups, you will be able to identify which category a given student falls into. When you subsequently set tasks that require collaborative work, make sure you have a mix of ideas, intellect and people-oriented thinkers in each group.

ACTIVITY

Discuss these three categories with your students to find out which type each student identifies with. Make it clear that we all have the ability to develop the other aspects in ourselves too.

We have now looked at a large number of thinking 'tools' that can be used as part of the in-forming process: the construction of a blueprint or map of how we think the world works, and how we as individuals fit into it. The map represents the basic understandings we use to survive and to flourish. 'Understanding' has been defined as *that which is under me as I stand* – the bedrock as it were formed from the meanings we have made, personally, culturally and as a species. It is much more, therefore, than a body of knowledge. I may 'know' that Paris is the capital of France. I may know millions of other things, but it is how I use this material that makes it powerful. Knowledge is power when it is applied.

The notion of the 'learning curve' is an interesting metaphor. I wonder how changing the metaphor would change a student's (or our own) perception of the learning process? My own favourite representation is a road: I speak of 'walking along the road to mastery'. In terms of skills we begin that road in a state of conscious incompetence. We consciously try hard to remember and do every part of the process so very carefully, usually with disappointing results – I only have to think back to my first driving lesson to know that this is the case! Through active engagement and regularity of practice we become consciously more competent, but remain subconsciously incompetent. Only when the skill becomes automatic, when we can consciously relax into a state of 'flow' that demonstrates our subconscious competence do we know that we have reached a high degree of mastery.

ACTIVITY

Take the opportunity to discuss the idea of 'learning' with your students. Mention the 'learning curve' and apply the PIN technique (Idea 80). Invite students to suggest other metaphors for learning.

THE LEARNING CURVE

Inventing is often classed as a creative thinking skill (see my *100+ Ideas for Teaching Creativity*), but actually the term is broad enough to include a more logical and systematic approach to the process. The use of the context grid in Idea 98, although relying upon the sudden insights that brainstorming can produce, also accommodates a step-by-step procedure towards the same outcome of developing something different or new.

The criss-cross technique exploits one aspect of inventing, that of combining two or more elements. The simple equation is 'cross A with B to get C'. So by combining a chair 5/6 with cushions 3/3 we not only reinvent beanbags but also, with a little exploration invent:

○ Zip-up cushion covers fixed underneath and at the back of the chair, which can be used for storage.
○ Electrically heated cushions for use in cold weather.
○ 'Vibro cushions', which may also be heated, to massage and soothe an aching back.
○ 'Sleep cushions', which release a soothing aroma and play soft music to ease away the stresses of the day.
○ Audiobook cushions, which read you a story when you sit on one and stop when you get off.
○ Videocushions – one example might show a map of the country. When you press one part of the map a voice gives you some information about that area.

ACTIVITY

Combine these items from the context grid and see what happens:

○ A brush 1/6 and a torch 3/6.
○ A book 6/2 and a wipeable surface 6/3.
○ A sticking plaster 3/4 and a microscope 1/5.

ACTIVITY

Invent new words by criss-crossing prefixes, roots and suffixes. Use these as appropriate to imagine new objects. For example, what do the following word-combos suggest?

○ aquarette
○ interport
○ cyberscribe
○ (to) octofy

WORD FLIP

The word-flip technique is not only a simple and fun way of developing inventive thinking, but it also encourages students to play with language, thus developing their 'linguistic intelligence'. This notion forms part of the psychologist Howard Gardner's so-called *multiple intelligences model* of how the mind works. Gardner asserts that rather than defining intelligence simply as the routine use of logical–sequential thinking skills and the ability to retain and reiterate factual material, it might be better imagined as the latent ability we all have to 'handle information'. That is, to manipulate and play with ideas across a range of domains on knowledge and understanding.

One of the intelligences that Gardner's work highlights is linguistic intelligence. This is not simply the ability to decode written and spoken information (which is functional or utilitarian literacy), but means developing students' potential to use language as a life-enhancing and life-transforming tool. The word-flip game is one technique for encouraging this.

Merely take a common expression, transpose the words and see what happens. So 'fridge magnet' becomes 'magnet fridge'. What new device does this suggest? What uses might it be put to?

ACTIVITY

Word-flip the following terms:

- car stereo
- tree house
- garden fence
- traffic light
- car park
- picture hook

IDEA
87

REPURPOSING

Repurposing is a process found in nature and a concept used in engineering, where something developed or designed for one purpose can be used for another. According to the mechanisms of evolution for example, scales became feathers and forelimbs became wings. Stone Age knives developed into scrapers, spears became arrows, wheels were repurposed as waterwheels, fireworks turned into various weapons, and so on (see David Perkins, *The Eureka Effect*, p. 19 – see Problems of Logic and Insight, Idea 76).

Repurposing can take place as the result of sudden insight, or might equally well come about through a deliberate search to find a fresh purpose for something that already exists. In his book David Perkins recounts the tale of an inventor working for 3M who was trying to develop a new kind of glue. The material turned out to be not very adhesive, so the question was asked 'What purposes can this (apparently useless) material be put to?' One solution is history, but I wonder how many more your students can think of?

ACTIVITY

Take one or more items from the following list and ask your students to repurpose them. It doesn't matter if students rediscover the wheel (as it were). The value of the activity is in deliberately looking at familiar objects in new ways.

- anti-vandal paint
- a motion sensor
- a thermos flask
- 'silly string'
- Blu-Tack
- a cork notice board

There are many kinds of creative excursions, which take us beyond the use of routine thinking into fresh areas where we may acquire new skills and/or combine and consolidate tools with which we are already familiar. Any creative excursion 'pushes the envelope' and presents challenges that draw us to the edge of our comfort zones and accelerate our journey along the road to mastery.

Use these problem-solving strategies with your students. In each case, first identify the problem to be solved.

o Choose a favourite animal and forge a link: an analogy, a personification, etc.
o Or select a character: from fiction, or a celebrity you like, or a historical figure. How would (s)he deal with it?
o Use a metaphor. If this problem were a feeling, how would I deal with it? If this problem were a household object, what solutions suggest themselves?
o Clarify the *domain* in which the problem occurs: work, personal life, technical, etc. Select another domain (a field of motifs) that interests you: the theatre, a hobby, some other professional field. Investigate ways in which problems are solved in this other area, then bring the insights and strategies back to your own difficulty and look at it with fresh eyes.

Effective thinking uses both conscious and subconscious resources. Conscious thinking is linear, logical, analytical; its agenda is 'out in the open', in present moment awareness, and amenable to change at will. Subconscious thinking is holistic, multi-tasking, symbolic/metaphorical and non-rational (in the sense that we might not be able to trace the reasoning behind creative leaps from one idea to another); its agenda is hidden. In the right mental state we become aware of the outcomes of subconscious thinking without necessarily having insights into the mental processes behind them.

Activities and techniques which foster whole-mind thinking are to be encouraged.

ACTIVITY

A particular example is to use a familiar short story such as Cinderella. Along the story-line mark the places where significant events occur: Cinders wants to go to the ball, the fairy godmother appears, she dances with Prince Charming, etc. Now at each point draw a line leading away and note an alternative scenario: Cinders receives offers for two parties on the same night, the fairy godmother does not appear, she does not much like Prince Charming, etc.

A bifurcation is a splitting into two. Have students draw a horizontal line to represent a 'straight forward' process. Draw a number of dots along its length to mark significant points in that process and/or places where another option or route is possible. At each node add a second line striking off at an angle. Each bifurcation creates the opportunity for an alternative option to be taken or another possibility to be explored.

Each alternative scenario can lead to further consequences. If you explore these a richer branching structure is created. This is the template for a decision tree.

A key feature of the thinking skills approach to teaching and learning is the use of tasks and activities that *actively engage* the mind in different kinds of thinking. Students whose thinking is reactive (guess the right answer), or who are expected to be passive recipients of knowledge, are not developing the powers of their mind.

A clear example of this distinction is the use of information presented in the form of a graph. Graphs are used in many school subjects and students are often asked to construct them. The task is frequently quite undemanding although the result looks impressive. In thinking skills' terms this is a dead graph, insofar as few thinking tools were actively employed in its creation and other students are not often required to interpret the graph's meaning or to challenge its implicit conclusions.

A 'living graph' seeks to encourage thinking in its construction and subsequent discussion. Have students work in pairs. Present each pair with ten statements in correct sequential order linked to the topic under study. Encourage the pairs to discuss which parameters will be chosen for the vertical and horizontal axes – the statements will give clues about these. Help students to decide where on the graph they will make a mark to position each statement. Present each graph with the ten statements to the rest of the class, but this time with them out of order. Have the class use the graph to decide on the order of the statements.

So, for example, here are ten statements in chronological order about the life of a hypothetical family:

DEAD AND LIVING GRAPHS

1 Ben Leech is born at the City General Hospital in Kenniston in December 1953.

2 Ben's father Steven Leech loses his job as a long-distance lorry driver when Ben is three years old.

3 Steven's wife Eleanor takes in laundry and sewing work to eke out Steven's inadequate dole money.

4 She continues to do this work for two years and the family gets by on her money.

5 In 1958 a new haulage company is established on the outskirts of Kenniston and Steven Leech is taken on as one of the drivers.

6 When Ben is seven years old his sister Katie is born.

7 Steven Leech takes a training course and six months later acquires the position of junior manager at the haulage company early in 1961.

8 When Katie is four years old her sister Lucy is born.

9 In 1966 Steven Leech is promoted into a middle-management position.

10 When Ben is 12 years old his mother has a big win on the Lottery and they move to Spain, where they live happily ever after.

Now imagine a graph where the horizontal axis is marked out in years from 1953 and the vertical axis is marked as a 1–6 scale representing comparative degrees of wealth. Plot the rise and fall of the Leech family's fortunes over the years by using the information from the ten statements. Now scramble the statements and ask students to arrange them in the correct chronological order by studying the graph.

Any concept map shows associations and relationships between motifs (constituent features) within a given domain. Help children to list motifs – for instance the events, characters and significant objects in a story – and represent each one as a key word/phrase or a simple picture. These are then cut out and arranged on a large sheet of paper, with plenty of space for the network of linking lines to be drawn. Children then annotate each line with a brief explanation of the link.

So, for example, within the domain (topic area) of the solar system, motifs would include the names of the planets plus other features: the Sun, moons, asteroids, comets, etc. as well as related concepts such as radiation, orbits, exploration, trajectory, folklore of celestial bodies, etc.

CONCEPT MAPS

THE THREE-COLUMN GAME

The Three-Column Game encourages lateral thinking, creative leaps and excursions.

o Make a template of three columns, with 11 segments in each column.

o Number the segments 2–12.

o Decide on three topics. These do not have to be within the same subject area. For example, household appliances, fantasy, the environment.

o Choose 11 motifs from each topic and represent them as a key word, phrase or simple picture. Motifs for household appliances could include vacuum cleaner, TV, can opener; for fantasy – wizard, magic wand, flying horse; from the environment – desert, water cycle, mountains, etc.

o Fill the template with the motifs placed in their respective columns.

o Ask students to roll two dice together for a number between 2 and 12. Repeat this for the other two columns.

o Select the chosen motifs and brainstorm links between them.

Playing the Three-Column Game can lead to some startlingly original ideas and underlines the creative principle that 'to have the best ideas we need to have *lots* of ideas'.

The game of 'What If' encourages prediction, speculation, creative excursions, philosophizing, problem-solving and the asking of open, divergent questions. Although the basic premise of each what-if can be fantastical (such as 'What if all colours changed once each year without warning?'), subsequent discussion is likely to focus on practical solutions to the problems raised.

When you ask any what-if, append three subsidiary questions:

o What might the world be like?
o What problems could we have?
o How will we solve those problems?

Some what-if scenarios that have worked well for me include:

o What if gravity switched off unexpectedly for ten minutes each day?
o What if, at the age of 30, people began to shrink, so that by the time they reached 75 they were only one inch tall?
o What if there was a non-human species that had evolved on Earth that had ten times our intelligence?
o What if time moved at different rates on each continent?
o What if wishes came true for one day only?

What-if stars offer a way of focusing discussion after a what-if question has been asked. Choose five topic areas, for example: school, travel, animals, shopping, politics. Draw a five-pointed star on a large sheet of paper and put one of the topic headings at each point. Write the basic what-if question in the middle of the star, and instruct students to jot down notes about the questions they ask and the solutions they reach.

WHAT IF AND WHAT IF STARS

Faction is a version of the What-If Game where the scenarios are more realistic – though it must be emphasized that the underpinning thinking skills and the themes and issues that are discussed are just as rich and valid however fantastical the proposition. Here are some Faction what ifs that have worked well for me:

○ What if wealth was redistributed evenly so that nobody owned more than anyone else, and everyone was paid a standard wage regardless of the job they did?

○ What if children could choose what they learned at school?

○ What if (for reasons to be discussed and decided upon) every husband had to have two wives, or vice versa?

○ What if computers replaced human judges in law courts?

○ What if the career that a child followed was decided at the age of five?

CUT-UPS FOR ETHICAL DILEMMAS

We have already met the cut-up technique in Idea 66, Cut-ups. The technique involves writing pieces of information on scraps of paper, which students then have to rearrange towards a specified goal. The immediate value of the cut-ups technique is that it encourages discussion and gives practice in organizational skills. Depending upon the particular task in hand the activity also highlights logical–sequential thinking and instructional writing.

ACTIVITY

A variation of the technique allows students to explore social and ethical issues. In this case choose a topic such as 'The town council intends to introduce car parking charges despite strong public opposition'. Ask students to create pieces of information relevant to the issue. These might be personal opinions, anecdotes, quotes from newspapers, statistics and other facts, etc. Some examples are:

- Car parking charges encourage people to use public transport.
- Philippa Stephens prefers using her car for reasons of personal safety.
- Traffic flow through the town has increased by 50 per cent over the past six years.
- Rail commuters and workers in the town will find free parking in side streets rather than pay hundreds of pounds a year to park 'officially'.
- Over the past decade motoring costs in 'real terms' have gone down, while travelling by public transport has become more expensive.
- A car-sharing website would be cheap to set up and would save many people plenty of money.

Generating some of this information provides a relevant opportunity for research. The number of cut-ups used will vary according to your time-frame and the depth to which you want the class to explore. When you run the activity suggest different ways in which the information can be organized – For and Against the proposition, sequenced according to perceived relevance or factual veracity, etc.

BEYOND THE FRAME

This activity employs a number of thinking skills to enlarge the context beyond the small piece of information that's given.

○ Choose an extract, perhaps a pageful of information, and centre it on a large sheet of paper.

○ Discuss the deeper structure of what's given with your students. Use the what-do-we-know triangle, the Star Check tool, analyzing for assumption and bias, etc. In other words, create an initial context by making explicit information 'enfolded' in the extract.

○ Explore the information that might have preceded what's given. In other words, what might the author have said leading up to the extract? Infer and deduce the points that logically should lead up to it. Sequence and prioritize your suggestions.

○ How might the author continue? Use bifurcations, decision trees, the If-Then Game, etc. to construct a logical sequence that follows on.

○ In certain cases, for instance if you are using an extract from a story, write a 'parallel extract' to the one given: If one character is featured in the extract, describe what another character who's mentioned but not present might be doing. In the case of non-fictional material, a parallel extract might take the form of the same information presented for younger readers.

Our conscious thinking operates in cognitive space, through time and at varying levels of detail. This is to say we are aware of those conscious thoughts, which move in a linear sequence from one to another. Sometimes we are aware of trains of thought and we can reflect on how our thoughts link together. Sometimes, however, our conscious point of attention seems to leap from idea to idea in a disconnected or even random way.

Activities like the Because Game, the If-Then Game, what-if stars, concept maps, etc. focus attention and create logical links in our thinking.

Another aspect of our moment-by-moment thinking is its 'chunk size'. Thoughts might take the form of a broad overview, or notice small details. Consider a novel you've read. You can survey the whole story in one mental sweep (large chunk), or recall vivid sentences and images (small chunks), simply by a flip of the imagination.

The While Game (for more about this, see *100+ Ideas for Teaching Creativity*, Idea 87) gives students practice in using this mental zoom tool. Another technique, the Chunking Triangle, makes the activity more systematic.

Draw an inverted triangle and mark it out into boxes (Figure 9 shows an example). The space at the tip of the triangle, at the bottom, gives enough room to write a few words which might be a theme, a topic heading, etc. This is the large chunk that can be systematically broken down into smaller pieces as you move from layer to layer towards the base (top, in this case) of the triangle. Reading the layers from left to right creates a sequence of ideas at that level.

THOUGHT LINES AND CHUNKS

Figure 9: The Chunking Triangle

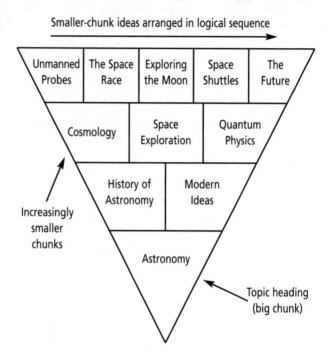

Context grids allow many motifs to be assembled and made available at a glance. Create a grid of, for example, six-by-six boxes. You now have 36 motifs which help to define and describe a topic/area of knowledge. Figure 10 shows a collection of household objects with a few (deliberately) ambiguous items thrown in. The immediate value of this *visual organizer* is that the students can see at once that all of these ideas are potentially related by being 'in the same frame'. Develop the use of the grid in various ways:

o Use the grid to practise co-ordinates. Move along the horizontal axis first and then up the vertical – 'along the corridor and up the stairs'.
o Choose two or more items and brainstorm ideas for new household gadgets.
o Extend the activity by using a greater number of motifs to create a concept map.
o Use the words and pictures to practise thinking skills such as attributing, comparing/contrasting/sequencing, etc.
o Use dice to choose two items at random. Notice how our minds put these two smaller 'chunks' together to create a bigger idea.

Figure 10: Context Grid

(Note: For further uses of the grid organizer see *100+ Ideas for Teaching Creativity*.)

MIND MAPS

The phrase and technique of 'mind mapping' was made famous by Tony Buzan. The visual networked structure of mind maps echoes the way in which we encode information in the brain, and features four key elements:

○ Different categories of information arranged in different parts of the visual field. So, for example, taking the topic of 'pet care' ideas about choosing a pet might go towards the top of the sheet, ideas about shopping for a pet might go on the left hand side of the sheet, ideas about caring for your pet might go at the bottom of the sheet, etc.

○ These different categories of information are colour-coded for ease of reference.

○ Key words tag the categories e.g. Pets – choosing, finding, care, etc.

○ Creative and logical links are then made between the categories to enrich the network of relationships and help create an overview.

ACTIVITY

○ Use a number of motifs from the context grid (Idea 98) to practise Buzan-style mind mapping.

○ Select motifs from the context grid and invite students to link them together at various levels or 'chunk sizes'. For instance, they all come under the topic heading of Anglo-Saxons. This is a big chunk idea. Smaller chunks might be family, military, agriculture, adornment, etc. Use Venn Diagrams to arrange these ideas visually.

○ Draw a circle. Insert a number of motifs from the grid. Say to the class, 'These are all thoughts going on inside the mind of an Anglo-Saxon (warrior, farmer, etc.). Why is (s)he thinking about these things, and why is (s)he thinking about them in this way?' The activity encourages creative linking and invites interpretation. Add a few 'wild cards' – motifs from other areas – to make the game more interesting.

A simple and effective way of familiarizing students with mind maps is to use a picture as a visual analogue. As an example we'll use the image overleaf – *The Walker*, by artist Chris Pepper. (This same picture appears in *100+ Ideas for Teaching Creativity*, where other ways of using it are explained.)

ACTIVITY

Place the picture in the middle of a large sheet of paper. Ask students to make observations about it. If a student, for example, notices the rats in the bottom right-hand corner, use 'rats' as a colour-coded key word towards the bottom right of the large sheet. Any other information pertaining to the rats will be written in the same colour around the key word. So items like 'I heard that in cities you are always within 2 metres of a rat' or 'Maybe there's rotting food nearby' or 'In the Middle Ages rats carried bubonic plague' will cluster around the key word 'rats' towards the lower right of the large sheet.

PICTURES AS ANALOGUES FOR MIND MAPS

'The Walker' © Chris Pepper

The word 'theme' comes from the Greek and means 'something laid down; to place or set'. Themes are the 'big-chunk building blocks' we lay down first as we construct our understandings. Unlike blocks, however, themes are not static things. They are processes acting like powerful undercurrents as we build our day-by-day experiences into an overall impression of the world.

Thinking on the basic level of themes effectively draws together and makes sense of the many disparate elements that make up our lives.

Themes tap in directly to our sense of who we are, to our identity, attitudes and fundamental beliefs about life. The themes we live by (intentionally or otherwise) can limit or liberate. Reflecting on themes allows us to work with them more deliberately. They often appear as metaphors and in the generalizations we use. It was only in adulthood that I came to realize that themes I kept returning to in my fiction were also important in my life generally:

○ Stepping over the line
○ The thought of forbidden territory
○ Randomness or design in the universe
○ Actions and consequences
○ Transformation, directed and undirected, control and happenstance

If we subscribe to the thinking skills approach to learning, then one of our goals must surely be to give children the capability of thinking at this level and having influence over the themes that frame their lives.

ACTIVITY
○ Discuss how the themes that interest me might have some relevance to the students' own lives.
○ Brainstorm ideas for using these themes in stories of different genres.
○ Explore how these and other themes might apply in different subject areas: science, history, geography, stories and poems, etc.
○ When students become more familiar with the concept of themes, encourage them to identify other themes that are personally significant.

THEMES AS INTEGRATING FORCES

The compartmentalization of knowledge into subject and topic areas is a logistical and administrative convenience in schools but does not truly reflect either the way the world works or the way in which the human brain learns – essentially by making connections. The educationalists Neil Postman and Charles Weingartner in *Teaching as a Subversive Activity* point out that the psychological phenomenon they call 'hardening of the categories' inhibits flexible thinking, natural curiosity and exploring 'outside the box'. The very use of the metaphor 'box' implicitly acknowledges this idea.

The greater danger inherent in a hardening of the categories is that it leads to the development of mind-sets, by which I mean 'minds *set*'; fixed ways of looking which can increasingly deny fresh ideas and reject other viewpoints. Any educational strategy which acts against this tendency must be positive and healthy.

Cross-curricular work in schools encourages students to appreciate the interrelatedness of knowledge. Usually the links are made at the level of themed content. In a primary school I visited recently Year 2 was spending a whole week studying the Anglo-Saxons. Lessons in English, maths, history, geography and science focused on that topic area. There was a real 'buzz' of interest about Anglo-Saxons in the air.

ACTIVITY

Cross-curricular links can, however, be made at a deeper level. 'Big themes' go to the roots of the human condition. Consider how these examples span subject boundaries and might be explored through literature, science, etc.:

○ Fair dealing is preferable to treachery.
○ The downfall of the proud is inevitable.
○ Accumulating wisdom outwits oppression by the powerful.

Or take a 'Big Picture' idea such as *wealth*. Discuss its meaning with students and explore how it relates to what they are learning about in their different subject areas that week.

ACTIVITY

Thinking skills themselves are common to all areas of knowledge. Take a simple thinking tool such as attributing (Idea 41). Encourage students to apply that kind of thinking in every lesson they take over the next few days.

MOTIFS

We have touched upon motifs a number of times in this book so far. They are the constituent features that help to define and describe a larger domain. In a sense they are the individual jigsaw pieces that combine to turn a puzzle into a completed picture.

ACTIVITY

○ Take a topic or subject area and invite students to list motifs that contribute to it. These will largely amount to the 'vocabulary of the subject'. Create a concept map using the motifs (see Idea 91). Have students link motifs and annotate the linking lines to explain the relation and/or highlight areas where confusion still exists.

○ Create a visual organizer as in Idea 98 filled with motifs from your topic or subject area. Use random dice rolls to choose pairs of items and encourage students to suggest links between them.

The most successful thinking, in my view, is that which unites motifs and themes into a meaningful whole. Classroom exercises that keep these things separate, that are partial and fragmentary and compartmentalized, run counter to the ethos of the thinking skills approach.

Using this book effectively, then, means creating strategies – selections of tasks and activities – that draw together different thinking tools so that small ideas can be combined into more general understandings. The philosopher A. N. Whitehead made the point that 'we think in generalities but we live in detail'. For me the greatest value of teaching thinking is to offer ways of linking the large and the small, the themes and the motifs to create meaning at every level.

VIVID PARTICULARITIES

'Vivid particularities' are details of our experience that create a powerful impression. They deliver a strong emotional impact and often embody a startling metaphor, or may represent an original or unusual creative link. They are, as it were, the grains of sand around which our larger meanings form. For these reasons vivid particularities represent a powerful technique for teaching and learning.

Develop the habit of noticing the particular and the striking in your subject area. Encourage your students to pick out vivid details of their experience. Build these into the teaching and learning environment. Use them to anchor learning experiences linking themes and motifs within domains of knowledge.

o My A-level biology teacher once said that sea anemones stuck to rocks when the tide's gone out look like 'half-sucked wine gums'.

o The scientific visionary Carl Sagan argued for nuclear disarmament and highlighted the fragility of the Earth by saying that if all of our nuclear weapons were launched simultaneously (in the early 1980s) an atomic explosion would ravage the face of the planet 'once each minute down all the hours of a long sunny summer afternoon'.

o The astronomer Tycho Brahe lost his nose in a swordfight and had a false one made out of gold.

o D. H. Lawrence in the final scene of the book *Sons and Lovers* describes the character Paul Morel as 'one tiny upright speck of flesh, less than an ear of wheat lost in the field'.

ACTIVITY

Ask students to think back to striking moments in their lives and, as appropriate, share these with the group. Mention learning experiences from your own schooldays that made a strong impression on you. Ask students about pieces of information they remember really clearly and why these things linger in the memory.

Bringing it all together

Good learning habits are established when the what, how and why come together through regularity of practice, driven from within by curiosity, encouraged from without by at least two presuppositions:

o Students already have all the tools in the mental toolbox.
o Expectations determine outcomes.

The 'what' of learning in terms of content has long been prescribed for us, but simply 'knowing facts' does not amount to understanding. Indeed, it has been caustically but perceptively suggested that 'mere coverage is the death of understanding'. If facts are to be taught, then in terms of a thinking skills approach they are best communicated with 'how' and 'why' in mind.

Successful teaching and learning displays the qualities of sincerity and authenticity. Sincerity means having the attitude you want the students to have – showing curiosity about the world, noticing, questioning, selecting the kinds of thinking that continue the in-forming process.

Authenticity means:

o Setting tasks that the students perceive as relevant to the real world, against a background of key ideas and principles (the domains of knowledge and understanding that Howard Gardner calls the 'natural intelligences').
o Allowing students to take on responsibility for their own thinking in an environment where ideas are valued. This boosts self-confidence and self-esteem (how we estimate ourselves).
o Establishing a true sense of achievement by both student and teacher setting high standards through mutual agreement.

ACTIVITY
Review some of the tasks that you have recently set, or intend to set, for your students. Assess them against the above criteria for authenticity. Subsequently, ask your students to go through a similar review. If some of the tasks emerge low on the 'authenticity rating', how might they be raised?

The 'traffic lights' metaphor of understanding is well known:

- o   Red – I don't understand and need help.
- o   Amber – I think I understand and have tried to use this idea, process, etc.
- o   Green – I understand this idea and think I've used it successfully.

This technique can be developed by adding more steps:

1   I don't understand this idea/technique and I haven't used it.
2   I think I understand this idea and I've tried to use it.
3   I do understand this idea and could explain it to someone else.
4   I can/will use this idea in other areas of this subject.
5   I know how to use this idea in other subjects at school.
6   I know how to use this idea in other areas of my life.

ACTIVITY

In collaboration with your students, create a list of tasks, concepts, techniques, etc. that have formed part of their recent learning. Introduce the 1 to 6 scale of understanding and have students begin to match the list against the scale. Develop this review by using 'Concept Pie' explained in Idea 107.

A 1 TO 6 SCALE FOR UNDERSTANDING

Develop the 1 to 6 scale of understanding and application by using a 'Concept Pie'. Draw a circle and divide it into a number of 'slices'. Each slice represents a concept, technique, process or component of learning. For instance to check back on a student's writing you might earmark the following: punctuation, spelling, neatness, research, bias and logical structure. Annotate the pie with these elements, and instruct the student to make a mark in each slice depending on how well she thinks she's done in that area. Use the 1 to 6 scale of understanding, where 1 is at the centre of the circle and 6 is at the rim.

It is interesting for you to review the same piece of student's work using an identical template. Compare results. Then ask, 'What clues did I notice in this work that has led me to these conclusions?'

Review the work, amend the Concept Pie if appropriate and then encourage the student to ask these two vital questions:

○ What changes would I need to make in this work to move the marks closer to the edge of the pie?
○ What have I learned by doing this piece of work that will make my next piece of work even better?

In the 1950s Benjamin Bloom developed what he called a 'taxonomy of thinking', which classifies levels of thinking from simple mentation where some knowledge is retained but there is little understanding, through to highly complex processing where synthesis of a great deal of information occurs leading to greater understanding.

Some commentators on Bloom's work suggest that it is a misinterpretation to believe that thinking evolves in a ladder-like way from simple to complex or that, by the same token, younger children or 'less able' students cannot accomplish more complex thinking tasks like evaluation, analysis and synthesis. I want to add that conventionally work on thinking focuses on conscious processes and omits or undervalues the subconscious resource. Furthermore, understanding can occur as a series of illuminations (see Idea 11) which are the outcomes of subconscious in-formation. Bloom's taxonomy seems not to include this vital aspect of subconscious synthesis.

Nevertheless, Bloom's ideas form a useful tool in assessing the sophistication of a student's thinking. Basically the hierarchy consists of:

o *Knowledge*. Recall of facts and ideas
o *Comprehension*. Basic understanding of ideas and the ability to put into other words
o *Application*. The use of knowledge or skills in a different situation
o *Analysis*. Understanding *structures* of knowledge and ideas: seeing the bigger picture through relationships
o *Evaluation*. The ability to use criteria to assess: using criteria and reasoning to support a judgement
o *Synthesis*. The creation of new or original ideas

ACTIVITY
Use a variation of Concept Pie (Idea 107) with your students that incorporates Bloom's taxonomy. Invite students to talk about their areas of interest, hobbies, etc. and help them to notice any higher order thinking they bring to their chosen topic.

BLOOM'S HIERARCHY OF THINKING

ON THE SHOULDERS OF GIANTS

Synthesis can be taken to mean the creation of something new and useful out of what has existed before. Original ideas and perceptions arise from the soil of earlier thinking. Isaac Newton supposedly and famously stated that his groundbreaking ideas occurred to him because he stood 'on the shoulders of giants'. Originality necessarily involves the accumulated wisdom of others coupled with a student's willingness to explore, question, doubt and suggest alternatives. This requires a diverse range of thinking tools rooted in the creative attitude of being prepared to 'go beyond the given'.

All of the ideas in this book are intended to contribute towards that goal. By absorbing others' points of view the student, with encouragement, can develop a viewpoint that is at least his own and may be fresh and insightful on the larger scale.

ACTIVITY

Take an issue such as 'This country's power needs in the next century'. Create a range of viewpoints – What would a conservationist think about this? How would a shareholder in a gas company react? What does someone from the pro-nuclear lobby have to say? Ask students to adopt a particular outlook (which need not be their own) and gather facts and opinions that support that position. From this platform of information, have students devise at least one workable (and perhaps fresh) strategy for dealing with the issue.

The heading for this idea comes from the poem of the same name by Wallace Stevens. The poem itself will repay any time you spend rereading it and quietly contemplating its depths. More immediately, it offers up an insight for practising flexible thinking.

THIRTEEN WAYS OF LOOKING AT A BLACKBIRD

ACTIVITY

1 Choose an object and have each student in the group write one statement about it. In a class of nine-year-olds I worked with we chose 'dog'. Some of the 'ways of looking' were:
   - Big, small, laid back or excited, but always your friend.
   - Sniffs out drugs and brings them to the uniformed man.
   - Only bites your hand when he's cross.
   - Howls when his owner has gone.
   - Chases cats, but only because people expect him to.
   - Top dog, underdog, dog-tired, dog eat dog – but all just dogs really.

2 Step 1 demonstrates many viewpoints. Using the same theme or another one, have each student think of several statements that look at the theme in different ways. In a class where we chose 'water' one eleven-year-old girl wrote:
   - Earth crying through loss.
   - Hydrogen and oxygen in a certain arrangement – but it still tastes sweet!
   - Some people would give their souls for a drink of it.
   - All the oceans made out of countless raindrops.
   - Mars is so alien – not a single tumbling stream.
   - Cycles endlessly, renewed and returning. There's a lesson here.

3 Rehearse the multiple-viewpoints strategy wherever possible. Guide students' thinking by asking 'How would a scientist look at this? How would an optimist look at this? How might you look at this in thirty years' time?'

HIGHER ORDER THINKING, LOWER ORDER THINKING AND FUN THINKING

It is easy to make value judgements about the terms 'lower order' and 'higher order' thinking, especially if we passively accept received wisdom and fail to challenge its (or our own) inbuilt interpretations of such ideas. Thinking is always complex and my own approach to developing thinking skills bears in mind the following:

○ *Challenge the metaphor*. If I realize that I interpret a hierarchy of thinking as being like a ladder, I can alter my perception by changing the metaphor so that thinking becomes a box full of tools, a map where all places are connected, a wizard's castle where magic happens – whatever serves my goal.

○ *The nature of the understanding*. We have already touched upon Professor Kieran Egan's idea that, as they develop, children understand the world in different ways. Young children 'mythologize'. If a young child explains that the sun rises every day because God kicks it like a football across the sky and spends the night looking for it, then rather than insisting that's wrong and correcting the child, I can recognize it as a wonderfully original 'naive theory' and celebrate the achievement.

○ *Orders of originality*. A thinking skills approach creates opportunities for children to 'rediscover the wheel'. A child might come up with an idea that's old hat to me, but it's original to the child. That's the point. By encouraging individual originality I am helping to prepare the ground where ideas that are original to the world might germinate.

○ *Children love to think*. It is a natural human activity. When children feel safe and know their ideas are valued, they will increasingly become self-motivating and demand greater challenges.

ACTIVITY

Work with students to review a range of tasks and techniques you have used with them in their learning. Assess these with the above ideas in mind.

We all remember stories better than we remember lists of ideas. This is because stories are complex webs of ideas linked by a robust and ancient structure wired deeply into the brain.

NARRATIVE TECHNIQUES FOR EFFECTIVE LEARNING

The traditional way of teaching follows the pattern of Objectives–Content–Methodology–Evaluation. An alternative model for teaching and learning that integrates a thinking skills agenda explores knowledge as though it were a story. It has been called the *narrative dynamic* model and incorporates the following elements:

o   Orientation/Complication/Resolution
    -   Orient students within the domain to be explored. Connect the learning to establish the Big Picture. That is, set the scene.
    -   Pose a problem. The students as the 'heroes' of the story make a thinking journey to solve it. That is, they are required to use various thinking skills to reach a greater level of understanding.
    -   By overcoming obstacles, realizing dead ends, striking off in new directions, students eventually solve the problem, thus demonstrating that learning has occurred. For us as teachers it is a re-solution. We know that the answers have already been discovered, but the heart of the learning is in the students discovering the wheel for themselves.
o   Humanize the knowledge. Explore the people behind the knowledge we want the children to learn. Establish relevancy by having children link the knowledge to their own lives.
o   Use narrative techniques in communicating knowledge – tension, surprise, mystery, humour, emotive language.
o   Sprinkle vivid particularities through the teaching to make it sparkle.

(Sources: K. Egan, *Teaching as Story Telling*, University of Chicago Press, 1989. M. Tilling, *Adventures in Learning*, Network Educational Press, 2001.)

Explain the narrative-dynamic model to your students. Suggest that coming to understand something is like a story. We set the scene. We embark on a journey to know more, which involves tasks, challenges and problems. How we go about this leads to a (re)solution, where we know we have learned. Deliberately set students activities within this model of learning, where a range of thinking skills leads to solutions to problems.

I am repeating myself in mentioning now that in the right environment children will motivate themselves to think. Children love to think, explore, discover and explain. Here are a few specific strategies to aid the process:

○ Give the children notes, pictures, stories, essays, etc. containing deliberate mistakes and ask the students to spot them.
○ Leave out topic headings, story titles, etc. and ask the children to suggest some after you've explored the topic.
○ Give the students more materials, equipment, information, etc. than they need. Ask them to weed out what isn't necessary and prioritize what they retain.
○ Sometimes go beyond conventionality. Have students present their learning in different ways – knowledge set into a story, for example; experiments described through drama and role-play; essays about people written up as letters, diaries, shopping lists, etc.
○ Stop in the middle of a story, experiment, topic and ask children what might happen next.
○ List and celebrate children's good thinking behaviours.

A MELANGE OF MOTIVATORS

Suggest to your students that when they need to write in their workbooks, they 'write on the right-hand page, while the left is left for notes'. Left-hand pages can be used for preparatory work, first-draft sentences, preview comments by yourself and the student, feedback and commentary while the writing project is ongoing, and review comments once it is completed, including the use of the 1 to 6 scale for understanding.

A variation of this idea is 'writing between the lines', where students are encouraged, as they compose their work, to write a line then leave a couple of lines blank before writing the next line. Again this gives room for word-by-word commentary on the project.

Both of these methods result in more valuable educational documents, insofar as they show both the finished product and something of the process that went on in its creation.

As we have seen, two fundamental questions that need to be asked during a review are:

○ What changes must I make for this to be the best work I can do today?
○ What have I learned by writing this project that will make my next work better?

The questions listed in True, False and Dare (Idea 33) can also be applied at this stage, together with these tasks:

ACTIVITY

Giving your students guidance as necessary, have them select:

○ An extract from a textbook
○ One or more pieces of their own recent work
○ A piece of another student's work (with their permission of course) and carry out the following:
  – Paraphrase any sentences or paragraphs you aren't happy with. Decide why exactly you think they are not satisfactory.
  – Draw out the main idea from each paragraph and suggest at least one reason why it is important.
  – If the work is arguing a case, take a different perceptual position and make notes for a counter-argument.
  – Be aware of any strong positive or negative emotional responses you have to the work. Pin down what has caused that reaction.
  – If you disagree with statements in the work, list reasons why. If you agree with statements, can you find reasons additional to those that the author has expressed?
  – List any further questions arising from the work.
  – Note any personal experiences linked to ideas found in the work.

A RANGE OF RESPONSES TO INFORMATION

Another measure of a student's understanding is the degree of conventionality found in his or her work. Conventions are the frames within which a project is given structure. Conventions of genre refer to the ways in which the motifs/vocabulary of a subject are traditionally used and combined. Conventions of form dictate how the outcomes look.

'Right answers' tend to be convention-bound. There is nothing wrong in this per se. We need to learn the rules well before we can begin to question and go beyond them. Answering comprehension questions and writing up observations of experiments follow a set pattern for reasons of logic and clarity. On a broader scale, aspiring writers, musicians, artists, etc. will often imitate their creative heroes. Sometimes they never go beyond that and remain watered-down copycats of more powerful and original voices. Occasionally the mimic phase is just that, a necessary stage in the development of the artist's own distinctive style.

Conventionality is useful while it serves practical purposes. When it limits thinking and creativity it has become another kind of 'hardening of the categories'. At the heart of the use of conventionality lies the notion of *intention and effect*.

When I write I have one or more intentions in mind. I intend that my readers will make sense of what I say. I intend to create the opportunity for illuminations and realizations to occur. Certainly in fiction I intend to evoke a range of emotional responses. It might well be argued that the most powerful art – indeed the most powerful communication of any kind – happens when the effects it has on the recipients match the communicator's intentions.

As teachers advocating a thinking approach to learning, we should therefore look for conventions of genre and form in our students' work, but encourage and value work that, when appropriate, 'goes beyond the given'.

ACTIVITY

Select an extract from, for example, a novel, a textbook, or select a poem or a newspaper article, a painting from a particular school of painting, a piece of jazz music, etc. and ask students to explain how they *know* it is jazz, pages from a textbook, etc. In other words ask them to isolate some of the aspects of genre (kind) and form that mark out the piece under review.

ACTIVITY

Follow this up by your students studying music, art, writing, scientific theories, etc. that were or are regarded as *un*conventional. Select examples of genius and 'crankiness' to encourage students to think about how people decide which is which.

SEVEN DISPOSITIONS FOR EFFECTIVE THINKING

The writer and educationalist Guy Claxton prefers to speak of 'dispositions' rather than 'skills', a term he finds to be somewhat cold and mechanical. A skill has been defined as 'thoughts embodied in action'. Skills, therefore, are the outcomes of thoughts rooted in the tendencies we have to behave in that way. Such dispositions, therefore, are broad and vague and originate in us at a deep level.

The seven dispositions listed below summarize the attitude we recognize in effective thinkers. When I meet a number like this I am reminded of what Somerset Maugham said: 'There are three golden rules for effective writing, and nobody knows what they are.' Sound advice, because first there are as many effective strategies as there are effective writers, and to put a number on it can limit thinking beyond that number. So take what follows as a moveable feast and feel free to add to the list.

Effective thinkers:

o Are adventurous, playful and curious;
o Like to wonder, probe, and enquire;
o Actively construct explanations (at their current level of understanding);
o Make plans and create strategies and are prepared to change them;
o Are precise, organized and thorough, even while recognizing that the creative aspects of thinking can be 'messy' – non-linear, irrational, metaphorical;
o Value ideas, seek and evaluate reasons;
o Are reflective and metacognitive.

ACTIVITY

Ask students first of all to reflect on their own attitudes and learning behaviours as measured against the list above. Work with students to discuss how learning tasks can encourage these dispositions even further.

Effective dispositions for learning can be drawn out and thinking skills sharpened by creating the right environment, a key component of which is you, the teacher, and the attitude you display. As you succeed in your aim, you are likely to notice positive changes in the behaviour of your students.

○ They will become more confident, less defensive, less prone to want to grab hold of right answers.
○ The dispositions reflecting effective thinking will be more in evidence.
○ Students will become more self-motivated in their approach to tasks and activities, and more self-directing in attaining their goals.
○ Language will change and become more overtly the language of enquiry. Students will ask more, and more searching, questions.
○ Perceptions will be less rigid. Opinions and standpoints will be defended rationally but not at all costs. The views of others will be respected.
○ Students will more competently apply the way they think to the task in hand, knowing when to take note of subconscious insights and when to use more consciously applied rationality.
○ Students who flourish in the environment you have established will relish challenge, love to think, celebrate their own and others' achievements and reach higher levels of attainment.

UNLOCKING LEARNING

ATTAINMENT AND ACHIEVEMENT

I am a writer. I write a book and submit it to a publisher. It is rejected swiftly and dismissively. I have not attained acceptance and publication, but my achievement has been to sit down and write that book.

I am an Olympic sprinter. I run in the Olympics and come fourth. My attainment did not even put me in the medals, but my achievement has been years of dedication, hard work and resiliency.

I am a teacher. One of the students in my class leaves school with a few low-grade qualifications, but says on departing, 'I really liked being in your class. You treated me like a human being. I want to train to be a teacher.' In this case my achievement is incalculable.

The above are based on personal experience (apart from the Olympic sprinter example). They illustrate the vital difference between attainment and achievement. We live in an educational world of levels and attainment targets: it's easy to lose sight of the achievement that might lead only to modest attainment. But all achievement is to be valued if the dispositions for effective learning are to be drawn out in our students.

ACTIVITY

Get students to draw a triangle and mark off the 'peak'. This is the attainment/achievement template. For a given piece of work, write the attainment score, level, etc. at the top. Use the rest of the triangle to list the student's achievement. Value it as well as evaluate.

Once students are familiar with this strategy, encourage them to list their achievements that lie behind each attainment.

'Out of clutter find simplicity. From discord find harmony. In the middle of difficulty, find opportunity'. Albert Einstein

'We learn what we do'. Marshall McLuhan

'Reason must have an adequate emotional base for education to perform its function'. Plato

'When the mind is at sea, a new word provides a raft'. Goethe

'Reality consists mainly of exceptions to the rule, which the intellect then reduces to the norm'. Jung

'When someone points at the moon, the fool looks at the finger but the wise one looks at the moon'. Traditional Chinese saying

'Someone who carries his own lantern has no need to fear the dark'. Traditional

'All things linked are. Thou canst not stir a flower without troubling a star'. Francis Thompson

'To remain a pupil is to serve your teachers badly'. Nietzche

'We struggle not to win or lose, but to keep something alive'. T. S. Eliot